*"To understand Volvo's future,
 you must first understand its history!"*

Volvo cars

– a cavalcade –

1927–2000

Christer Olsson

*Photographs by:
Hans Christiansen and others*

Translated by Tom Byrne

Norden Media GmbH

ISBN:
3–907153–01–4

©

Christer Olsson & Norden Media GmbH
1999/2000

First printing 1999
Second printing 2000

Published by:
Norden Media GmbH
St. Gallerstrasse 41a
CH-9034 Eggersriet
Switzerland
Tel. +41-71-877 36 84
Fax: +41-71-877 37 84
e-mail: sgnorden@bluewin.ch

English translation:
Tom Byrne, Techtrans Ireland, Cork

Repro:
ReproAteljén AB
Skövde, Sweden

Printed by:
G. Canale & C. S.p.A.
Turin, Italy

Contents

- Foreword — 6
- Preface — 8
- The founding fathers — 10
- A name and a symbol — 12
- Prologue — 14
- Debut of the Swedish car — 16
- Style and power! — 20
- 'Streamlined' model of the future — 26
- The first 'small' Volvo — 30
- The classic Volvo taxi and the first terrain vehicle — 34
- Fit for a King! — 36
- 'The people's Volvo' — 38
- 'The Sow' — 46
- The Duett – two for the price of one! — 48
- A plastic beauty – the Volvo Sport — 52
- Immortal two-tone beauty — 56
- Refinement — 60
- Most beautiful Volvo ever? — 62
- Safety and prestige — 68
- Safety first — 72
- Dutch town car — 74
- An enduring legend — 76
- 'The Flying Dutchman' — 80
- The taxi as fine art — 82
- Electric 'mini-Volvo' — 84
- Project 1155 — 86
- World's lightest Volvo — 92
- Springboard — 94
- End of an era — 98
- New generation — 102
- Ecological high-tech — 108
- An everyday racer — 110
- Two noble beauties — 114
- World's safest car! — 120
- Volvo 2000 — 124

Foreword

This new volume on the history of Volvo cars in the 20th century appears at one of the most exciting periods in our company's history.

Less than a year ago, Volvo Car Corporation became part of the Ford Motor Company, the biggest automotive group in the world.

Volvo Cars enters this new phase in its history with confidence, self-belief and pride in what it has achieved since its first car left the works on Thursday, 14 April 1927.

Leafing through the book, I am reminded, with pleasure, of the some of the Volvo cars which I saw on the roads in my younger days – models such as the PV60, PV444, Amazon and P1800.

Most people have a very special relationship with the car as a link with different events in their lives – their childhood years, their first car, family holidays, and so on.

I am also struck by the rapid pace of technical development and by how much progress we have made in the last few years alone. Cars such as the Volvo C70 och S80 offer tangible evidence of this.

We at Volvo Cars have a duty to remember our history and our roots. The 'Swedishness' of our brand is a quality on which we must build – and is one that I know our new owners are anxious to preserve.

I believe that this fine book will be appreciated by all who have a special affection for Volvo in their hearts.

Tuve Johannesson
President and CEO
Volvo Car Corporation

Preface

Volvo enters the 21st century stronger than ever, armed with a competitive product range, and with a skilled and dedicated workforce. Since the beginning of 1999, the company has been part of the successful Ford Motor Company, a guarantee of stability and long-term access to major development resources.

The fact that the Volvo name is now stronger and more respected than ever is not attributable to recent developments alone; today's Volvo cars trace their origins back more than seventy years, to the era when a few pioneering souls with limited resources, but sustained by a common vision, came together to build a car suitable for Swedish motorists and Swedish conditions.

The story is now familiar; one of the world's leading makes of car was born with a capital of SKr200,000, which was not a huge sum in an industrial context, even in the 1920s. The first open-top model was built in just over 200 examples; today, any one of Volvo's plants around the world can produce the same number in an hour.

Very little was known of the history of Volvo and its cars when I began first began to research the subject in 1976 (in preparation for the company's 50th anniversary in 1977). The founding fathers had consistently ignored the past, urging their colleagues to 'think ahead' and to get rid of all their dusty old documentation. This regrettable attitude, which was shared by Assar Gabrielsson and Gunnar Engellau, has unfortunately made it difficult – if not impossible – to reconstruct the company's history.

However, interest in the subject on the part of innumerable Volvo enthusiasts around the world has grown steadily, in contrast to the lukewarm interest displayed (even until recent times) by AB Volvo and its subsidiaries. Thanks to these devotees, many thousands of now-classic Volvo cars have been found, restored and preserved, with the result that early Volvo models, such as the PV444, PV544, Amazon and P1800, are now a common sight both in 'informal' veteran car rallies and in 'serious' classic car events. Unfortunately, older pre-1950 Volvos are still rarely seen, although both these and later classics from the 140, 160, 240 and 260 series are re-emerging as time goes on.

The restoration of growing numbers of classic Volvo models is not the only way in which the company's history is being brought to life. Realising the importance of that history – especially as a source of inspiration to its employees – Volvo management has begun to see the company's 70-year traditions in a new light and has invested new resources in it. The museum based on the collection of Volvo cars assembled over the years by Svante Mannervik was established during Gunnar Engellau's tenure. This collection, supplemented by later Volvo products, is now housed in the fine Volvo Museum at Arendal, outside Gothenburg – a 'mecca' for all Volvo enthusiasts lucky enough to visit it.

Very little was written about Volvo until about twenty-five years ago. Since then, however, historians, authors and journalists have made significant efforts to chart its history, and Björn-Eric Lindh, in particular, carried out invaluable research into the history of the cars as part of the company's 50th anniversary. Very many people could be named in this context. To avoid omissions, I shall refrain from mentioning them all, although two individuals – Peter Haventon and Bengt Sahlström – occupy a special place. As researchers and writers, both made an outstanding contribution by dispersing the mists surrounding that history. Neither should Rolf Illermark's dedicated documentation work be forgotten.

Despite Volvo's long indifference to its own history, the flame was kept alive by the staff of at least one department at the company's corporate headquarters in Torslanda – the Volvo Central Archives – where I have enjoyed more than twenty years of amicable cooperation with (in chronological order) Lars Sjöberg, Olle Högberg, Ingrid Alexandersson, Ulla Bergwall, Ewa Persson and Göte Jönsson. Without their untiring efforts to maintain the archives, Volvo would have been the poorer for loss of valuable historical documentation. To these, I owe a major debt of gratitude, not only for their work in preserving the records, but also for their constant assistance in helping me to locate documents and illustrations for the four books on Volvo's history which I have been privileged to write and publish between 1987 and 1999.

My particular thanks are due to Kjell Hansson (who managed the Volvo competition workshop during its halcyon days in the 1960s, when Volvo triumphed in a series of European championships) and to rally driver Carl-Magnus Skogh. Both of these gentlemen helped me to record Volvo's exciting history in competitions, which will also be the subject of a special volume planned for publication in autumn 2000.

I am indebted to Christer Weiss, acting historian of Volvo Car Corporation, for his help and encouragement with the project. Christer also contributed the quotation reproduced on the frontispiece of this book.

I would also like to thank Anders Kull and Bengt Lennerbert of Volvo Car Corporation, who contributed pictures and are still helping me to record Volvo's modern competition history.

One man deserving of my especial gratitude is Bosse Gullbrandsson, without whose support this volume would probably not have seen the light.

However, history need not be confined to musty old documents and old, black-and-white pictures. In this volume, therefore, these are supplemented by beautiful new photographs of elegant cars.

Some motoring historians are antipathetic to new pictures of old cars. To them, history is a thing of the past, to which nothing can be added. I do not subscribe to this view. In some instances, the cars depicted in the new photographs have been lovingly restored to their original condition, a credit not only to their owners, but also to their families and all who have helped to recreate a particular part of Volvo history in this way.

For this reason, I would like to direct a very special 'thank you' to the owners of the cars pictured in the new photographs which adorn many of the pages in this book. These include Ulf Olsson (ÖV4), Bernt Olsson (PV4), Kjell Olsson (PV652 & PV36), Jan Hillgren (PV654), Thomas Söderberg (PV655 cabriolet), Anders Nilsson (PV51), Hans Böttner (PV56), Evert Jonasson (PV822), Thomas Hådell (TPV), HM Carl XVI Gustaf of Sweden (PV60), Frits Bernats (PV444, PV444BS & PV444LS), Lennart Pettersson (PV444AS & PV445 cabriolet), Bert Andersson (PV444HS), Gunnar Nilsson (PV832), Swedish Army, Södermanland Regiment (TP21), Gunnar Blomquist (P1900 prototype chassis), Rune Svensson (P1900), Leif Strand (P120 Amazon) and Jan-Olof Klerehag (PV544). Particular thanks are due to Boo Brasta and Heinz Linninger for their valuable assistance in arranging the photograph of the royal PV60, and Ulf Nielsen, who arranged the picture of the P1900 chassis prototype.

I would like to record my particular gratitude to Hans Christiansen, whose photographs of the restored cars expresses their individual 'spirits' in a manner which I believe is unique in Sweden. However, this is not surprising given that Hans is not 'merely' a photographer, but also a dedicated car enthusiast.

The attractive photographs of the PV655 Cabriolet are the work of Bengt Svensson, while the impressive pictures of the TPV and TP21 were taken by Roland Brinkeberg.

Although writing a motoring history is a stimulating task, it can be difficult to interest publishers in what is a specialised area and very few authors are lucky enough to find a publisher who shares their enthusiasm for projects of this nature. It is my good fortune to have, as publisher and friend, Sven-Erik Gunnervall, a man who combines publishing experience with an enormous interest in history of all kinds – including that of cars – and, above all, is dedicated to the production of *beautiful* books.

It would be impossible to write in depth about a company such as Volvo without assistance in recording its current history, and I wish to pay special tribute to Per-Åke Fröberg of Public Relations at Volvo Car Corporation for his help in this regard.

I mentioned earlier that Volvo has, at times, taken little interest in its own history. However, the importance attached by Volvo's present management to tradition, experience and history, as major factors in the success achieved by the company to date, is recognised in the foreword contributed by Tuve Johannesson, current president of Volvo Car Corporation, to this book. I thank him for his support which, I hope, will serve to remind his colleagues everywhere that the company's successful global operations today are founded on the contributions made by earlier generations of Volvo people.

Chambourcy, 5 October 1999

Christer Olsson

The founding fathers

The story of how Assar Gabrielsson and Gustaf Larson met by accident at Urbans café in Stockholm and how they later decided – over a meal of crayfish at the Sturehof restaurant – to start a company to produce cars, has often been told. It was a daring move at the time, given that many others had failed in similar ventures and that Scania-Vabis had only recently discontinued it modest production of luxury private cars.

The story probably contains elements of fiction as well as fact. In all likelihood, the two had already discussed the issue and they had certainly examined its feasibility, although it is not clear which of them had actually conceived the idea. Although Gabrielsson, as the 'real' founder of the company, is generally credited with it, there is strong case for believing that the origins of Volvo are actually attributable to Larson. Gustaf Larson had a long-standing interest in cars, having worked with a supplier to the industry in Britain, and designed a car engine himself

However, Gustaf Larson lacked both capital and contacts, whereas Gabrielsson had just received a 'golden handshake' from SKF (the Swedish Ball Bearing Company), where he had made himself unpopular with some members of management for dealing with the new regime in the infant Soviet Union. With a high reputation in business and banking circles, he would certainly have been receptive to a proposal by Larson to launch a new era in Swedish car production.

So who were these two men?

Assar Gabrielsson (1891-1962) was a native of Korsberga in Västergötland province, a tiny community located just outside Tidaholm which, from 1903 to 1934, was the centre of a successful truck and bus manufacturing operation. He was the archetype of an English gentleman, smoking cigars

Gustaf Larson (with his family) pictured behind the wheel of one of the GL prototypes.

and encouraging his colleagues to play golf, even during working hours!

Gustaf Larson (1887-1968) came from Vintrosa in the province of Västmanland. Unlike Gabrielsson, he was a rough diamond with a sense of humour which was by no means always benign. However, his often coarse manner was outweighed by his engineering expertise. His technical intuition was legendary and he was seldom wrong. One glance at a sketch was sufficient for him to assess the merits or otherwise of a design. And on the rare occasions that he was wrong, he still got his way; nobody dared contradict Gustaf Larson!

Although Gabrielsson and Larson were very different individuals, they shared one characteristic – loyalty to their friends. One result of this was a tendency by one to hire new employees on vague terms, often against the wishes of the other. This sometimes created problems for the new appointees, such as an American-based engineer who was engaged by Gabrielsson – only to be advised by Larson to move on 'to a hotter place'!

There was, however, one major difference between the two; Gabrielsson was the one who provided the investment capital, while Larson was actually the company's first employee.

A major achievement, the development of the first Volvo car 'from scratch' was not the work of Gabrielsson and Larson alone. Others deserving of mention in this context include the young engineer, Henry Westerberg, who carried out much of the draughting work almost without pay (he was later to become employee No. 1), artist Helmer 'Mas-Olle' Olsson (1884-1969), who was responsible for the styling of the first model (ÖV4), and Axel Roos, who was in charge of production of the prototype bodies at the well-known bodybuilding firm of Adolf Freyschuss in Stockholm. (Roos was later to be employed by Volvo in Gothenburg, a sure sign that he had rendered significant service to Gabrielsson and Larson during the company's first years in Stockholm.)

Assar Gabrielsson.

A name and a symbol

ÖV4 (1927).

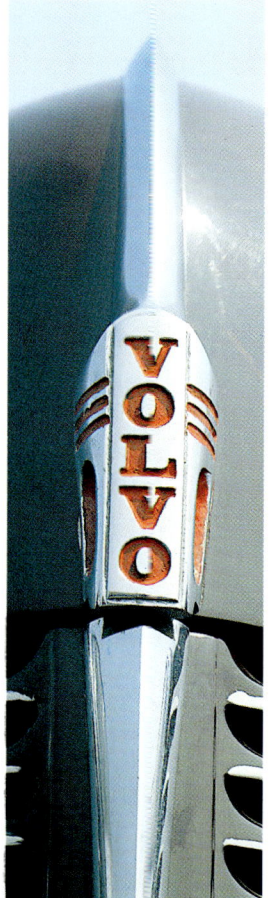

PV60 (1946).

PV802 (1938).

A new Swedish car, which was to be delivered to its first customers about a year later, was finally built by summer 1926. As yet, however, the model had no name and its 'manufacturer' was a private individual (Assar Gabrielsson), rather than a formally established company.

Gabrielsson availed of his excellent relations and standing with his former employers to acquire a dormant SKF company named AB Volvo, which had been founded in 1915. The deal included an abandoned factory site on the island of Hisingen, north of the city of Gothenburg. (Known locally as 'Nordkulan', this had originally belonged to a now-defunct competitor of SKF.)

In autumn 1926, the handful of people involved in the new project transferred their activities from Stockholm to Gothenburg. The 'Volvo' name was adopted officially and the company was formally reborn as a carmaker in August 1926.

In the company's advertisements, the new car was promoted as a Swedish car built for Swedish conditions, and it seemed appropriate to devise a company symbol which would reflect its Swedish heritage.

Since the car was built of Swedish steel, it was natural to adopt the recognised symbol for iron, which is also the symbol for the planet Mars.

The choice may have been influenced by the fact that the symbol had long been used to advertise and market Tidaholm vehicles, especially since these were manufactured a mere 15 km from Gabrielsson's parental home.

Although Gabrielsson and Larson were certainly the two most influential people behind the choice of symbol, the car's stylist, Helmer 'Mas-Olle' Olsson, would also have been involved in its design.

Since it seemed incongruous to mount the little badge on its own on the radiator, the latter was provided with a diagonal bar to which the emblem was attached. Thus, the famous Volvo diagonal 'stripe' was born – not as a decoration, but as a mounting device!

The iron symbol was to adorn Volvo cars for many years to come. It disappeared in 1944 and did not reappear until the US version of the PV444L was launched in 1957 (or, in the rest of the world, until it was displayed on the PV544 in autumn 1958). It was subsequently superseded once more – this time by a 'B18' badge – but returned in 1968 on the new 164, complete with the classic diagonal (which had been absent on the two abovementioned models). Since then, it has been a permanent feature on all Volvo cars, the latest version (on a blue background) appearing in summer 1998.

The symbol did not disappear completely from Volvo vehicles during the 1944-57 period, but continued in use on the company's trucks, buses and agricultural tractors. Although both it and the diagonal have been modified several times, the Volvo name – written in the 'Egyptian' typeface with its characteristic square serifs – has remained almost unchanged

Today, the Volvo name is one of the most respected and best-known in the world. To car enthusiasts, the iron symbol represents the values on which the Volvo company is founded.

PV544 (1965).

1800E (1969).

1800ES (1971).

S80 (1998).

Prologue

In 1925, those 'in the know' in motoring circles were suggesting that a new Swedish car was on the way. However, this was based mainly on rumour and most observers shook their heads knowingly; Scania-Vabis was just then in the process of shutting down its car production in Södertälje, while the Thulin (a copy of the German AGA), which was produced in the factory built in Landskrona by the now-deceased aviation pioneer, Enoch Thulin (1881-1919), had proved a failure.

The confusion began to clear in mid-1926. One of the first to cast light on the matter was John Nerén, the legendary motoring journalist, who reported that the new model was to be a Swedish quality car, designed in Stockholm and equipped with an open-top (cabriolet) body styled by the renowned artist, Helmer 'Mas-Olle' Olsson (who was often regarded as the heir of the celebrated Swedish painter, Anders Zorn).

The first pictures of the car were published in spring 1926. Secrecy was tight and the model still lacked a name. The Swedish public was not particularly fascinated; the car was a conventional (bordering on old-fashioned), five-seat, open-top model which was obviously designed to be reliable and rugged rather than exciting. The power unit was a conventional, four-cylinder, 2-litre engine with a rating of 25-30 hp, driving the rear wheels through an unsynchronised, three-speed gearbox.

The elegant body boasted simple lines. It was built, in the classical manner, of sheet steel on an ash frame. The nine open-top prototypes built in 1926 were finished in different colours, probably to distinguish them and to facilitate the choice of colour to be used on the production model, manufacture of which was to commence in 1927.

The first prototypes bore the name 'Larson' or 'GL'. Although the initials are commonly assumed to have been those of Gustaf Larson, they may equally well have stood for 'Gabrielsson-Larson' – although the truth will almost certainly never be known.

The later versions of the nine prototypes bore an increasing resemblance to the series-produced ÖV4 as aesthetics gave way to practicality – not an unusual occurrence in such cases. Although taste is always subjective, the more sweeping lines and smaller doors of the first prototypes were certainly more attractive than those of the series model which, in some respects, represented a departure from the stylist's original concept.

As the first 'offspring' of a relatively inexperienced design team, the GL was a fairly mature product. Apart from minor styling changes, redesign of the engine and relocation of the petrol tank to the rear of the chassis, it was generally similar

Test resources at the new Volvo factory were modest! The picture shows a stability test in progress.

1926–27

to the series models which were subsequently to be produced for the best part of two years.

Since the fledgling company was short of money, despite the support which Gabrielsson had received from SKF, it was decided not to scrap the prototypes on completion of testing, and most were sold at a lower price than the ÖV4. One was retained at the factory and fitted with a small platform for light transport duties.

Just one of the prototypes has survived to the present day. This was bought by SKF's industrial photographer, Sven Sjöstedt (who also worked for Volvo and took many of the pictures in this book). In time, he donated the car to the Gothenburg City Museum, where it can be seen to this day.

In 1926 and 1927, the prototypes were test-driven over long distances by both men and women.

Debut of the Swedish car

An ÖV4 (above) and a toy model by Somerville of Britain (below).

Swedish manufacturers are now among the world's leaders in the fiercely competitive medium-class car segment, in which comfortable, versatile and economical models must be marketed at reasonable prices. Both Swedish carmakers, Volvo and Saab, have travelled a long way to achieve this eminence – a journey which may be said to have begun on 14 April 1927, when the first series-built Volvo left the 'assembly line' at the Hisingen factory.

To be truthful, the first Volvo was by no means exciting in technical terms, based as it was on proven (i.e. obsolescent) technology. However, the care with which it was designed and built laid the foundations for the reputation of quality, durability and reliability which Swedish cars have enjoyed ever since.

In functional terms, the ÖV4 ('ÖV' was the Swedish acronym for 'Open car', while '4' denoted four cylinders) was hard to beat. Although the overall length was relatively short, the driver and four passengers travelled at a speed of 70 km/h in spacious conditions. The headroom was particularly generous; since the car was an open-top model, the sky was literally the limit!

The ÖV4 was one of the models which brought to an end what is usually known as the 'vintage' period of the car. Unlike today's models, it was built on a frame, with the body (which was not designed to be load-bearing) mounted on the chassis. Equipped with side valves, the engine rating was a modest 28 hp, while the gearbox provided only three (unsynchronised) forward speeds. The brakes were mechanical and acted only on the rear wheels, although the option of mechanical brakes all round did become available to buyers towards the end of the production period. In harsh weather, comfort was provided by a hood. The plastic side windows were attached separately (and were anything but well sealed).

Nevertheless, despite (or, indeed, thanks to) its primitive construction, the ÖV4 won the affections of Swedish motorists, who wanted a rugged Swedish car built to withstand the atrocious Swedish roads and the tough Swedish climate.

Unfortunately, however, the car was relatively expensive at SKr4,800 and sales were slow. One of the main reasons was the open-top design, which made the model less than ideal for use in Sweden all year round. Gabrielsson and Larson had opted for this type of car not merely for its attractive appearance; they also entertained hopes of selling it

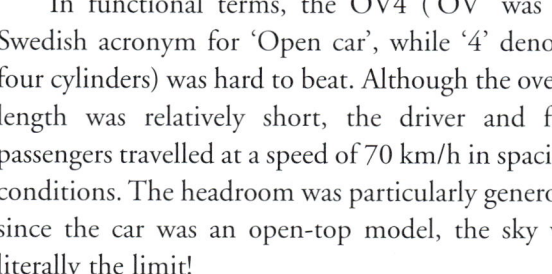

1927–29

Motoring trips could be adventurous, even in the 1920s.

in numbers in warmer countries to compensate for the decline in sales in Sweden during the winter season.

At the time, Sweden was a poor country with a badly paid working population (which, in itself, was essential to the viability of indigenous car production). Since the domestic market was small, it soon became clear to Volvo management that the company would have to move upmarket, producing bigger and more expensive models if it was to achieve success.

It was decided, therefore, that future models would be stronger, faster and more powerful – and capable of competing with their foreign counterparts.

Left: Beautiful natural materials, such as wood or leather, were used in many 1920s cars.

Bottom left and below: The Volvos of the 1920s were large handcrafted.

The model pictured on these pages is the first version of the Volvo PV4.

It was only a matter of months before the company introduced its second model. In technical terms, this was identical to its predecessor, the main difference being the completely new body. The attractive ÖV4 was now complemented by a less elegant, but more practical, covered, four-door model of a type which was to become the standard for comfortable family cars for the rest of the century.

The lines of the PV4 ('PV' stood for 'Passenger car') were less striking than those of the ÖV4 due, perhaps, to the fact that they were not the work of 'Mas-Olle' Olsson, but of the team responsible for the design of the model as a whole.

In fact, the covered model should have looked altogether different. 'Mas-Olle' had also submitted design sketches for an elegant, covered body consisting of an ash frame clad with sheet steel. However, this version (which was used on just one of the ten prototypes built in 1926) proved too rigid for the relatively weak chassis and the alternative of a 'semi-rigid' Weymann body was chosen instead. This differed from the conventional construction of the day in that it consisted of a timber frame covered with imitation leather (or genuine leather as an optional extra).

For a number of reasons, the PV4 and its successor, the Special, were the first and last Volvos with Weymann bodies. One of the main reasons may have been that moisture tended to penetrate behind the covering, causing the frame to rot.

The first PV4s were delivered in summer 1927 and sales, although better than before, were by no means exceptional. This may have been due to the relatively ungainly body shape and a new version, the Volvo Special, whose styling was more reminiscent of the sweeping lines of the open-top model, appeared in autumn 1928. Although this was also a Weymann type, the bonnet was lengthened at the expense of the rest of the body, making the car 'long' rather than 'high' (and making it appear faster than it actually was). The Special also featured a bigger, rectangular rear window, unlike the oval window in the PV4.

Since Volvo was still a tiny automaker, cars could be built to individual customer specifications. Perhaps the most spectacular variant produced at the time was a version of the PV4/Special referred to the 'Commercial Traveller', the rear of which was provided with a large opening door (hinged at the side rather than the top), effectively making it Volvo's first estate model!

Since these were the days before the motel, the facility of making up beds in the PV4/Special was a highly practical feature which Volvo proudly advertised in its sales brochures.

Model	Period of manufacture	Number built	Wheelbase, cm	Track width (front/rear), cm	Swept volume, cm³	Engine rating, hp	No. of forward speeds
ÖV4	1927–29	302	285	130	1,944	28	3
PV4/Special	1927–29	694	285	130	1,944	28	3

Style and power!

The photographs on these pages are of a restored Volvo PV652.

Volvo survived its first decades thanks only to the popularity of its trucks; sales of the four-cylinder ÖV4 and PV4/Special cars were much lower than company management had originally hoped. However, this problem had been foreseen for some time. The minutes of a board meeting held at the beginning of 1926 record that what the company really needed was a bigger, more powerful, six-cylinder model. This would attract buyers in the relatively high price class in which Volvo would have to compete to finance the high development and production costs involved in building quality cars.

The demand for higher power was not confined to the cars. The company's trucks, which were to be equipped with the same engines as the cars for several years more, needed a more powerful unit with at least six cylinders (an eight-in-line type was also considered).

Signs that Volvo was designing a more powerful six-cylinder car were perceived at the end of 1928 and the beginning of 1929 when ÖV4s with extended bonnets concealing the new engine began to appear on the competition circuit. Activity at Hisingen was intense; the company had survived the early years, and the market was now demanding 'finished' cars with top-class qualities and no weaknesses.

The new six-cylinder Volvo finally appeared in spring 1929. Technically, the new model was identical to its four-cylinder predecessor, although bigger and more rugged in design, while the engine was basically the same as its four-cylinder cousin, although with a slightly larger bore.

The new model bore the designation PV651 (the figures denoting 6 cylinders, 5 seats and version 1). Compared with its four-cylinder predecessor, it was a more modern car of exceptionally solid construction, with the unmistakably elegant and modern 'Mas-Olle' lines.

The brakes were still of fairly rudimentary

design, mechanically operated and acting on the rear wheels only. However, a model with hydraulic brakes on all four wheels (PV652) was introduced the following year (and PV651 owners could have their brakes modified to the new, improved type).

The technical details of the PV652 were largely unchanged, although a 'freewheel' was available to enable the car to coast downhill, helping to reduce engine wear and fuel consumption. However, this also increased brake wear and prevented the use of engine braking.

Unlike the previous model series, the enclosed version was now the main option, although an attractive cabriolet was available to customers who preferred that type. This was based on the PV650 chassis, which was sold in parallel to customers who wished to add their own custom-built bodies, or to build a commercial vehicle, such as a small pickup truck, van, ambulance or hearse. The cabriolet (actually a drophead coupé with winding side windows) was now an extremely luxurious car (an early forerunner of C70 Convertible of the 1990s).

Taxi owners were a group which soon took Volvo cars to their hearts. By 1930, they could already buy a 'stretched' TR version of the model ('TR' stood for 'Trafikbil', the Swedish equivalent of

'PSV') with space for more than the normal complement of four or five passengers. The TR models were available for many years both as city taxis (with an interior partition) and as country taxis (without a partition). At that time, taxis were recognisable by their attractive, dark-blue finish.

Two taxi versions were available initially: the TRS/TR671 (city version) and the TRL/TR672 (country version). Apart from their longer wheelbase and the extra, folding seats between the front and rear seats, these were identical to the ordinary cars.

After a year or so, both of the first taxis were replaced by the TR673 (city) and TR674 (country).

With its new six-cylinder series (and its taxis), Volvo had at last succeeded in developing cars which were attractive to growing numbers of upper medium-class customers. This was the category which offered the company the best potential of establishing its own customer group – buyers who attached greater importance to high quality and comfort than to low price or low fuel consumption.

Perhaps more than any other, the 1930s was the decade in which car design was brought – if not to a fine art – at least from a state of rudimentary simplicity to one of stylish functionality. Square shapes, defined by horizontal and vertical lines, were

The colour photographs on these pages are of a PV654. The model in the black and white picture is a PV653.

refined to produce rounder contours and body lines which ran diagonally, rather than horizontally or vertically, relative to the longitudinal and vertical axes of the car. However, Volvo was not yet ready to break completely with 1920s design and opted, in 1933, to introduce modified versions of the PV650 and 652 models (and the corresponding taxis).

The modifications to the new PV653 versions were much more comprehensive than suggested by a casual glance. The entire body had been basically redesigned and now featured rounded corners, while both the front (where the radiator still lacked a protective grille) and the windscreen, which had been almost vertical on the previous models, were gently sloped. The sweeping lines were reflected in the air vents in the bonnet, which were now inclined at a slight angle to suggest speed.

For the first time, Volvo now exploited the opportunity of increasing its sales revenue by tempting buyers with a 'luxury' model (PV654) with a more lavish standard of equipment. In addition to two spare wheels and twin horns, this also boasted more exclusive interior trim and more expensive upholstery. Whereas most standard PV653s were finished in black, the PV654 was available in a considerably more elegant dark-blue finish and an even more attractive wine red. Volvo's discriminating customers responded by buying the more expensive PV654 in significant numbers, giving a badly needed boost to the company's turnover.

Volvo's more attractively styled 1933-34 models also won the approval of Swedish taxi owners, who now had the option of a yet another body variant.

Volvo PV655 cabriolet.

Now known as the TR676, the high-bodied city taxi (which enabled gentlemen in evening dress to keep their top hats on!) was complemented by an extended country taxi on a 325-cm wheelbase, providing country folk and their baggage with even more generous space on their journeys to and from market or railway station.

In design terms, this body was, perhaps, the most successful of all the early six-cylinder cars. The increased length eliminated the vehicle's short, high appearance, conveying an impression of speed which the 65-hp engine was barely able to deliver to this heavy car. The extended taxi was available either with or without a glass partition behind the front seat in variants designated TR678 and TR679 respectively.

After a decade of existence, Volvo management was ready to cut the ties with the past and to develop new, up-to-the-minute models. Accordingly, plans were made to introduce 'the car of the future' in spring 1935. As always, however, Gabrielsson and, in particular, Larson were cautious and were not quite banking on the success of the new 1936 model with the buying public. Although the company did have its trucks (and, for about the last year, its buses) to fall back on if it lost the loyalty of its car customers, the main concern of the two was to make Volvo a make of car to reckon with.

In a space of about six years, Volvo had begun to be recognised as a quality marque, thanks to its big, durable, six-cylinder cars. Two groups in particular had taken the company's cars to their hearts: a conservative middle class and taxi owners, who appreciated the quality and space of the taxi versions. For this reason, the fact that the new, 'streamlined' model, with its lower overall height, would not be suitable as a taxi was almost certainly a crucial factor in the decision to introduce a last generation of 'conservative' models. These were to replace the PV653-654 and TR675-679 series in production for another few years.

The styling of these 'transitional' models represented an interesting compromise between the relatively square lines of the late 1920s and the progressive, 'streamlining' trend of the 1930s (although the last of the family was distinguished by relatively straight lines, these ran diagonally).

The front of the car was the main section which was modified, the most important innovation being the addition of a protective grille in front of the radiator. The 'streamlined' shape was suggested by making the grille pointed and steeply sloped. To ensure that the rest of the front section was in harmony, the wings were also redesigned and the air vents in the bonnet sides were inclined at a 'speedy' angle.

Mechanically, the 'new' models were practically identical to their predecessors, although the engine was more powerful and more reliable than before. Developed primarily for the new 'streamlined' car, but used in both cars and trucks, the new EC engine was to become a classic. With the benefit of an additional one-third of a litre of swept volume and an extra twenty or so horsepower, the new series models were livelier than before, although still more sluggish than their more powerful American competitors.

In practice, the choice of models was the same as before. Private car buyers had the option of the standard PV658 (which replaced the PV653) or the deluxe PV659 (for the PV654).

Taxi owners still had several variants to choose from, both for urban duties over short distances and for rural service carrying a half dozen passengers. With its short wheelbase, which facilitated driving in narrow streets, and its tall, old-fashioned body, the TR701 was the main option for the first application. The country models were the TR703 (with a glass

A model car (by Brooklin of Britain) based on the TR704.

The Venus Bilo, the functional 'concept car' built by Volvo as a 'prototype' of the revolutionary PV36 (see pages 26-29).

partition behind the driver) and the TR704 (without a partition). These came with a longer and lower body, with adequate space for (at least!) six passengers on the three rows of seats (including the folding seats between the normal front and rear seats).

Fastidious buyers who wanted a body custom built by one of the independent coachbuilders still in existence had the choice of two chassis lengths – an option availed of by customers including HM Gustaf V of Sweden, who ordered an open 'hunting' model from Nordbergs in Stockholm.

Model	Period of manufacture	Number built	Wheelbase, cm	Track width (front/rear), cm	Swept volume, cm^3	Engine rating, hp	No. of forward speeds
PV650–652	1929–33	2,382	295	142	3,010–3,266	55–65	3–4
TR670–674	1930–34	659	310	142	3,010–3,266	55–65	3–4
PV653–655	1933–35	653	295/355	142	3,266	65	3
TR675–679	1934–35	186	310/325	142	3,266	65	3
PV657–659	1935–37	542	295/355	142	3,670	80	3
TR701–704	1935–37	936	310/325	142	3,670	80	3

'Streamlined' model of the future

The photographs on these and the pages overleaf are of the PV36. Below, right: A model car based on the Mars, a 1930s marque.

While the updated PV658/659 and TR701/703/704 series were extolled in Volvo's brochures and in *Ratten* (the company's customer magazine), it was the 'streamlined' PV36 which was the big news from Volvo in 1935. For the first time, company management felt that Volvo was in the forefront of automotive development, and could compete with American, British, French and German makers in building the most modern of cars. Truth to tell, however, the advertising claims were exaggerated. Although the new model (which was soon nicknamed the 'Carioca') was admittedly modern in its styling, it was still built on a heavy, rugged frame (of almost truck proportions). As a result, its performance was mediocre, especially in comparison with ultramodern models such as the Citroën B7/B11 'Traction Avant', which had been introduced a year earlier and which, with a monocoque body and front-wheel drive, already boasted features which would become standard several decades later.

Prospective buyers were certainly surprised by the radical design of the PV36 Carioca – and probably by its price of SKr8,500, which was substantially more expensive than other Volvos and other, competitive models in the same size class. The price, together with the native caution of the Swedes, meant that it took several years to sell the planned volume of five hundred PV36s.

In appearance, the PV36 was modern compared with its contemporaries. The styling was copied largely from the American Chrysler Airflow and De Soto Airflow models and, to some extent, from the Hupmobile Aerodynamic. This was not a new phenomenon; all automakers at the time copied from their competitors. The styling of the Chrysler Airflow set the trend for a year or so and even smaller cars, such as the Singer Airstream in Britain, were modelled on it.

All of these automakers found their customers just as indifferent as Volvo's. Sales of the Chrysler, De Soto, Hupmobile and Singer 'streamlined' models all failed to meet their makers' expectations, and all of the manufacturers reverted to more cautious styling for several years afterwards.

Although the lines of the PV36 were advanced for their time, the body was of conventional construction, consisting of a steel-clad, timber frame mounted on the heavy chassis. As a result, the kerb weight was high in relation to the relatively modest power developed by the six-cylinder, side-valve unit under the bonnet. The roof was still covered with imitation leather since the presses at Olofström (where the body panels were manufactured) were not sufficiently large to press the component in a single piece.

1935–38

The PV36 was more advanced than other Volvos in one respect; its independent front-wheel suspension enhanced the car's roadholding. However, since the design also made the front end both complex and expensive to produce, it was not until 1953 that it was used on big, six-cylinder Volvo cars (specifically the further developed version of the taxi).

Opinions of the PV36 Carioca vary. Most of those who have never actually seen or driven the model, but have only studied it in later years as a veteran car, tend to see it in the same rosy light as the P1900 (another of Volvo's glamorous mistakes). Past and present owners, on the other hand, have a more qualified view, regarding it as an overly expensive and heavy car, although offering a relatively high standard of comfort and generous interior space.

Model	Period of manufacture	Number built	Wheelbase, cm	Track width (front/rear), cm	Swept volume, cm³	Engine rating, hp	No. of forward speeds
PV36	1935–38	501	295	146/143	3,670	84	3

The first 'small' Volvo

The pictures on these pages show a restored PV51 and a contemporary cabriolet built on the PV51/52 chassis.

Nineteen thirty-six was a year in which no less than three different model series with five different bodies were produced by the little Swedish carmaker. In addition to the three 'conservative' models – the PV658/659, the short city taxi (TR701) and the extended country taxi (TR703/704) – the range included the exclusive (and expensive) PV36 Carioca, and the year's major news, the 'little' PV51.

Things were improving steadily in what had once been a poor country. In addition to a small upper class and a large working class, Swedish society now included a growing middle class, one of whose primary aspirations was to own a car. This had not escaped the attention of the country's Volvo dealers, who watched with envy the success of Adler, Citroën, DKW and Opel on the domestic market, without a small, economical Swedish model with which to compete. Another decade was to pass before the real answer to their prayers appeared; meanwhile, although the PV51 was no 'small' car, it was definitely a step in the right direction in the development of a car for the masses.

The plans to develop a model smaller than the PV36 were a couple of years old. Comparison between the revolutionary Carioca and the

outwardly, fairly conventional PV51 reveals that the similarities were greater than the differences. Both were built on a conventional frame and both were equipped with basically the same mechanical components. The two models also represented a radical departure from the 1920s styling which had characterised Volvo's models until then.

From the production engineering aspect, the PV36 and PV51 provided tangible evidence of a 'master plan' designed to make cars just as profitable to manufacture as trucks and buses. The ingenuity of this was highlighted by the fact that the engines were already used in the company's trucks and that most of the other components (with the exception of the frame, body and interior trim) could be purchased from external suppliers, placing few, if any, demands on development resources. Technically, however, the PV51 and its successor were less complicated (and less expensive) than the PV36. As an example, a

1936–45

The front underwent a major facelift in 1938 in keeping with contemporary design trends, and the styling became more angular. The model designations were now PV53 (replacing the PV51), PV54 (replacing the Special), PV55 (replacing the PV52) and PV56 (the deluxe version with the same rear end as the earlier Special). The PV57 chassis version was available to buyers wishing to add their own bodies.

The PV51-57 series was a major success. Several thousand examples were to be sold between its introduction and the end of World War II, many to the Swedish Defence Forces for use as staff and radio communications cars.

conventional beam front axle was used.

The PV51 was an excellent, if unspectacular car of rugged construction, with generous space for four to five people. Since it was powered by the same engine as the PV36, but was equipped with a smaller and lighter body, its performance was superior to that of earlier Volvo models.

In 1937, the solid, standard PV51 was complemented by a 'deluxe' version (PV52) and a 'Special'. The latter featured a more spacious boot with a well in the bottom for the spare wheel (which had previously been mounted externally).

All of the colour photographs on these pages are of a PV56 which has been preserved in its original, unrestored condition. The black and white picture of the period shows a producer gas car in a camouflage finish.

Model	Period of manufacture	Number built	Wheelbase, cm	Track width (front/rear), cm	Swept volume, cm³	Engine rating, hp	No. of forward speeds
PV51–52	1936–38	3,005	288	142	3,670	86	3
PV53–57	1938–45	3,900	288	142	3,670	86	3

The classic Volvo taxi and the first terrain vehicle

The need to offer the company's most loyal customer group – taxi operators – a more modern vehicle became acute in the mid-1930s. Although these had taken readily to the old-fashioned 'Volvo six', American cars were now superior in terms of both engineering and comfort. Furthermore, both the PV36 and PV51/52 had shown that the Hisingen factory could produce modern cars.

A truly modern, comfortable and attractive Volvo taxi was finally unveiled in 1938. This time, however, only one basic model was built for all types of duty. Equipped with a high, comfortable body for city use, the model was built on the same 325-cm wheelbase as the earlier TR678/TR679/TR703/TR704 country taxis, providing generous space for all passengers, even with the folding seats occupied.

In terms of styling, the new arrival was related to the PV53-57 cars, featuring a 'pointed' nose in keeping with the prevailing 'streamlining' trend. The impressive overall length of 530 cm was utilised to the full by extending the passenger space almost to the very rear of the vehicle. Baggage was accommodated in a high, but relatively short boot, with the spare wheel in a separate well underneath, in the same manner as in the PV51/52 Special and the PV54/56. If required, the partition wall between the passenger and luggage compartments could be made removable to accommodate a stretcher, converting the vehicle into a temporary ambulance.

In construction, the chassis of the PV801 (city version, with partition) and the PV802 (country version, without partition) was more like that of a light truck than a small car. This was intentional, since vehicles of this type were also used extensively as vans and ambulances. Bare chassis, both on a standard wheelbase of 325 cm (PV800) and in an extended 355-cm version (PV810), were produced for these applications.

The PV801/802 was a stable vehicle. Despite the use of beam axles, both the roadholding and comfort were of a high standard for the time, and were clearly superior to those of the earlier six-cylinder taxis.

For the first time, the body of a Volvo taxi was now made entirely of steel pressings, without a timber frame. As a result, the kerb weight was a 'mere' 1,800 kg, surprising low given the model's substantial dimensions and interior space.

The PV801/802 was used almost exclusively as a taxi (in a dark-blue finish). However, a few examples were built as company cars (some in an elegant maroon red) or as military staff cars (in a grey or camouflage finish).

In 1944, Volvo unveiled its first terrain model, which was essentially an all-wheel drive version of the taxi. Known as a 'TPV' (for 'TerrängPersonVagn', or

1938-48

'Terrain vehicle' in English), this consisted of a truck chassis with all-wheel drive, fitted with a taxi body with a foreshortened front (to improve terrain mobility). The steel roof was replaced by an opening canvas roof to provide the customary aircraft spotter with the best possible visibility.

The PV801/802 was produced in more or less unchanged form until 1948, although the modified PV801F/802F version (with a column gearchange) was introduced in 1946.

A final series with the same styling, bearing the designations PV821 (with partition) and PV822 (without partition), was produced in 1947-48. These models were powered by the more modern ED engine which, with the same swept volume but a somewhat higher compression ratio, was slightly more powerful than the EC unit. This last series of 'sharpnose' taxis was equipped with the same instrumentation as the PV60 (with what were popularly called 'Mickey Mouse' figures on the speedometer). In the last few years, the attractive dark-blue finish was replaced by black under new taxi regulations imposed by the Swedish government.

Below: A TPV terrain vehicle. Facing page, bottom left: A contemporary black and white photograph of a PV802 and its occupants. The other pictures on these pages are of a preserved PV822.

Model	Period of manufacture	Number built	Wheelbase, cm	Track width (front/rear), cm	Swept volume, cm³	Engine rating, hp	No. of forward speeds
PV800–810	1938–46	1,848*	325/355	147/152	3,670	86	3
TPV	1944–46	210	325	153	3,670	86	4
PV800F–810F	1946–47	*	325/355	147/152	3,670	86	3
PV821–824	1947–48	800	325/355	147/152	3,670	90	3

* Number includes both earlier version and later F version

Fit for a King!

The PV60 is not among the best known Volvo models, despite the fact that it was the last (and best) of the long series of six-cylinder, side-valve cars dating back to the 1929 PV651. The model was unveiled at the Stockholm Motor Show in autumn 1944, together with the Volvo PV444 'Peace Car'. As a result, it was overshadowed by its smaller sibling which, as events transpired, was to appeal to a much wider circle of customers.

The PV60 was a stable car which offered its propertied, middle-class buyers – who could afford to buy a car of this size by the late 1940s – a high standard of comfort. The bonnet concealed the 'new' 90-hp ED engine, a substantially modified version of the classic EC, whose origins dated back to 1935. The gearbox was still a three-speed unit, although overdrive was available as an optional extra. With the silent ED engine whispering discreetly under the bonnet, this made the model an even quieter and more comfortable touring car.

In appearance, the PV60 was certainly not ultramodern. However, its generous overall height afforded plenty of headroom, even for tall passengers wearing hats.

The relative anonymity of the PV60 today is remarkable, given that over 3,000 examples of the model were built in four years of production. Although Volvo now produces that number of cars in two days, a production volume of this order (at a time when materials, such as sheet steel, were in extremely short supply) represented an enormous step forward for the company as a carmaker. While Volvo had long been manufacturing trucks in thousands, it was not until the PV444 that it really became a mass producer of cars.

Production of the PV60 was started in 1946, the year that HM Carl XVI Gustaf of Sweden was born. His Majesty's 50th birthday in 1996 was marked by the presentation to him of a restored PV60, a gift from Swedish motoring historians which was much appreciated. HM Carl XVI Gustaf is patron of the annual 'Royal Rally', an event held each summer on the island of Öland, where Solliden, the summer residence of the Swedish royal family, is located. Together with his family, the monarch usually takes part in this event in his elegant PV60 (which is pictured opposite).

Most PV60s were supplied with the standard Volvo body. However, customers still had the option of a bare chassis (PV61), which could be bodied to individual requirements. The most beautiful examples of these special bodies were the attractive drophead coupés/cabriolets built by Nordbergs Vagnfabrik in Stockholm. While the small pickups or vans which were also built on the same chassis may not have been as ostentatious, they were equally serviceable. Custom-built 'stretch' taxis were also built on PV61 chassis for a short period between 1948 and 1950 (following the discontinuation of the PV821/822 and prior to the production of the PV831/832).

The PV60 was the last big, comfortable, six-cylinder Volvo car to be produced for a period of several years, during which the PV444/PV544 and

1944-50

Amazon provided the Swedish people with wheels. Just two decades later, however, another Swedish-built, six-cylinder model offering comfort rather than luxury was to see the light of day (see pages 70-71).

Facing page, bottom right: A black and white photograph of the interior of a PV60 (with its 'wrongly hung' rear doors). The colour pictures on this page are of the PV60 owned by HM Carl XVI Gustaf of Sweden.

Model	Period of manufacture	Number built	Wheelbase, cm	Track width (front/rear), cm	Swept volume, cm^3	Engine rating, hp	No. of forward speeds
PV60–61	1944–50	3,506	288	142/152	3,670	90	3

'The people's Volvo'

Below; The PV444 was the first mass-produced Volvo.

Bottom right: Many design models were made before the PV444 was introduced, including this one with front styling reminiscent of the Amazon.

Below: A true-to-life model of the PV444A by Somerville.

It was Assar Gabrielsson's vision that every man should own a car. During the first 15 years of the company's existence, however, he realised that this was no more than a pipe-dream; the man in the street did not yet have the economic resources to buy a new car, let alone a relatively big, robust, medium-sized Volvo. For two decades, therefore, the company lived mainly on its trucks, biding its time until sufficient numbers of Swedes could afford cars.

By the mid-30s, however, complaints from dealers were beginning to reach the company's head office at Hisingen. Small, economical European cars, such as Adlers, Citroëns, Opels, Peugeots and Renaults, had begun to outnumber the big US models. The Americans, in turn, had responded quickly to the challenge by producing small cars of their own. General Motors was already making Opels in Germany and Vauxhalls in Britain, while Ford was producing cars in Britain, Germany, France and Ireland.

It was time to develop a 'small' Volvo to complete the product range.

Initially, the designers had no idea how the car should look. However, they did have a name – PV40 – indicating both that it was to be a four-cylinder model and that it was to be introduced in 1940, together with the bigger, six-cylinder PV60.

1944-58

The first idea was to build a rear-engined model exactly like the new KDF-Wagen (otherwise the Type 1 Volkswagen) designed by Ferdinand Porsche in Nazi Germany at the behest of Adolf Hitler. This arose from the fact that Olle Schjolin, who was chief design engineer at the time, had brought home plans and sketches of similar (although bigger) American car powered by an unusual four-cylinder, two-stroke engine in a crosswise configuration. (This engine was often described incorrectly as an eight-cylinder since each of the four cylinders housed two pistons.) However, the idea was quickly abandoned, no doubt following evaluation by the shrewd Gustaf Larson.

It was soon decided to build a conventional model with a front-mounted engine (with overhead valves rather than the side valves which were a feature of all big, six-cylinder, Volvo car engines until 1957). Following the trend set by the small cars of the day, such as the Citroën Traction Avant/B11 and Hanomag, it was decided to develop a modern, monocoque body with independent front-wheel suspension – a formula which was to be a winner for several decades to come.

Designed to meet the expected requirements of young, postwar families, the new model had four spacious seats. In retrospect, the American-inspired styling was no surprise. American cars were popular in Europe, the leading Volvo designers had American experience and the USA was expected to enjoy the postwar gratitude of a Europe which owed its salvation from the excesses of Nazism largely to the American war effort.

Volvo's new little 'Peace Car' was unveiled with great fanfare in September 1944 in Stockholm (where the company's first prototype had been introduced 18 years before). It was an immediate hit. Like the ÖV4 seventeen years earlier, the price was SKr4,800 – a ridiculously low figure which barely covered the cost of production. As a result, large numbers of people signed contracts (many of which were later sold on at a handsome profit) to buy a car which would not be delivered until the end of the war.

The model bore the designation PV444 (as explained in *Ratten*, the figures stood for "4 seats, 40 hp and 4 cylinders"). A deluxe version known as the PV444AS was produced in 1950 only.

The PV444 finally gave Volvo several legs to stand on as an automaker. Trucks were already highly profitable and cars now began to follow suit as the rate of production of the PV444 increased (and especially when all of the underpriced 'contract cars' of 1944 had been delivered).

Although there was little reason to modify a successful model – especially when the only problem was to obtain sufficient steel to build the cars – it was decided to carry out the first revamp of the PV444 in 1950. As part of this, the model was renamed the PV444B (an 'A' being added retrospectively to the original 1944 designation).

Top and above: A preserved PV444A.

Overleaf: A preserved PV444AS.

This page: A beautifully restored PV444BS.

Although relatively minor, the modifications were important to a postwar public ready to forsake the motorcycle for the comforts of a car. The instrumentation which, following the British pattern, had formerly been grouped in the centre of the dashboard (possibly with the idea of producing a right-hand drive model), was now relocated in the driver's direct field of vision. The dashboard was also of a more austere, metallic appearance, in contrast with the green and white version in the original model.

Modifications to the exterior included two significant changes, most notably the replacement of the original, side-mounted, semaphore-type direction indicators by an indicator unit mounted on the roof. Destined to become known as 'the cuckoo on the roof', this odd-looking device was designed by Helmer Pettersson. Despite its disadvantages – its location in the centre of the roof made it difficult to see, it prevented the use of a roof rack and the roof had to be drilled to mount it – the feature was retained for a couple of years. However, a 'Q' model variant with conventional indicators was available as an option.

The bumpers were modified and the number plate transferred from its location on the boot lid to the rear bumper. The finish was still optional – provided that the choice was black (or dove grey if the buyer chose the exclusive deluxe model).

New, revised versions of the PV444 were introduced in time. Despite the criticism, the PV444C (1951-52) still featured the roof-mounted indicator unit, although the old-fashioned 16" wheels, with their four mounting nuts, gave way to the more 'modern' 15" type attached by five nuts. Although smaller, the new wheels still afforded excellent mobility on Swedish country roads, most of which had gravel surfaces at the time.

The PV444D (1952-53) was almost identical to the C series. However, life was made easier for the occupants by the provision of a specially designed heater (available only as an optional extra). Following many years of criticism, the 'cuckoo' was finally removed and replaced, on all versions, by side-mounted flashing indicators (although only after a change in the law and right in the middle of the production period).

'The people's Volvo' now acquired a serious degree of ostentation in the form of the incredibly elegant, maroon-red, metallic finish on the deluxe PV444DS. However, the cellulose-based metallic paint soon proved to be vulnerable to sunlight and faded in a relatively short time.

The PV444E (the last version with a divided rear window) was modified only in some details. However, the addition of heating as standard on later PV444Es was certainly welcome!

More important was Volvo's introduction of its 'PV Warranty' which, in reality, was a form of free insurance which the customer received when buying the car. Fearing a threat to their business, the Swedish insurance companies sued (and threatened Assar Gabrielsson with jail!). In the event, however, the matter was settled following protracted negotiations.

Today, new car models with new bodies are introduced at frequent intervals. Demands were not as high in the car-hungry 1950s and even small design changes hit the headlines in the motoring magazines.

The PV444H (and the deluxe HS) were greeted with considerable acclaim; the model had finally been comprehensively modernised. On this occasion, although the changes were modest, they were apparent to all. The most important and most

The PV44E was also exported to Japan.

In 1952, all Swedish children born in 1945 received a copy of the adventures of 'Willie Volvo' (a gallant little PV444) as a Christmas present.

Above: A Swedish 'Lucia' with a PV444L California.

Bottom right: Volvo PV444H.

Below: The PV444K adorned the 1956 Volvo road map.

visible modification was the large, single-piece rear window, which afforded better visibility and improved safety (although reversing was still a hazardous manoeuvre because of non-existent rearward visibility in the close-up zone). The restyling of the rear end was further accentuated by the relocation of the rear lights at waistline level.

The technical modifications, mainly to the steering and gearbox, were minor. The engine rating was increased from 44 to 51 hp during the production life of the H model.

A landmark event occurred in 1955, when the first Volvo cars in modern times were exported to North America. These featured the so-called 'American rails' on the bumpers and many boasted vinyl upholstery in bright colours. The bonnet concealed either the normal 51-hp engine or the B14A, a high-performance unit 'borrowed' from the P1900. This unit was sold only in North America, to the great frustration of speed-hungry PV enthusiasts at home in Sweden.

The Export model which was also introduced during the PV444H period was a less exciting car. Known as the HE ('H Export'), this was a 'budget' version with painted rather than chrome trim, without a heater as standard and with simplified technical features. It was not a market success and was discontinued after a couple of years.

The PV444K succeeded the PV444H at the end of 1955, when the ribbed grille which had been used since 1944 was replaced by a chromed 'grid' with projecting corners. Otherwise, the modifications were minor.

The L model (1957-58), on the other hand, underwent significant modification. The most important new feature was the new B16 engine, which was basically a B4B/B14 with a bigger swept volume and a higher output. The Sport version with twin carburettors was still only available outside Sweden.

Externally, the L model was distinguished by a new grille (the same as on the 444's successor, the PV544) with a large, golden 'V' in the centre. In the USA, a 'V' indicated that the car in question was equipped with a V8 engine, which was not the case with the PV444. As a result, the grille of the US version of the PV444L bore the iron symbol, which had not appeared on Volvo cars since World War II.

The combined direction indicator/parking lights were located at the inner side of the front wing (beside the grille) or to the outside on US versions. The rear lights were relocated on the rear wings and boasted a distinctive, yet elegant round shape.

The sporty, high-performance qualities of the PV444L were ably demonstrated by Gunnar Andersson, who took the 1958 European Rally Championship in the model (although photographs of his PV444L were often retouched to show a single-piece windscreen, the PV544 having been introduced by the time he won the title...!).

Above and left: Volvo PV444L. Far left: A model of the car.

Model	Period of manufacture	Number built	Wheelbase, cm	Track width (front/rear), cm	Swept volume, cm³	Engine rating, hp	No. of forward speeds
PV444	1944–58	196,004	260	128/130	1,414–1,583	40–85	3

'The Sow'

The PV444 was a success right from its introduction in 1944. At the same time, the highly popular PV800/PV820 series taxis were beginning to show their age and the obvious solution of resigning the 'sharpnose' front was adopted.

Introduced in 1950, the new series was to become loved and renowned under its apparently unflattering nickname of 'The Sow' (actually a reference to its rounded lines, which were reminiscent of a well-filled piggy bank!).

The PV831(city version, with partition) and PV832 (country version, without partition) were launched in summer 1950, and achieved immediate popularity due to their more modern looks. The first examples featured a number of chrome 'teeth' at the front; however, the classic PV444 look (on a slightly larger scale) was restored after about a year. The more exclusive and more modern appearance of the model compared with its predecessor was attributable to the new design of the front door, which now boasted quarter lights, and to the chrome trim along the sides. Inside, the 'new' Volvo taxi remained spacious and comfortable, with two folding seats for additional passengers between the ordinary front and rear seats.

In technical terms, the modifications were minimal compared with the last version of the PV821/822. However, a significant improvement was made in 1953, when the outdated beam front axle was replaced by more modern, independent front-wheel suspension.

Sales of the PV831/832 ceased in 1957 as

1950–58

interest in the series declined. More and more private individuals now had cars – not least in rural Sweden – and there was no longer a need for the huge taxis of earlier days. In addition, rising petrol prices, coupled with the advent of diesel taxis (such as the Mercedes 180D), had eroded Volvo's dominance in the Swedish taxi market. And now that the Amazon was about to be launched, there was pressure on production capacity in Volvo's plants.

A military terrain vehicle was also developed from the second generation of Volvo taxis. On this occasion, however, the extent of modification compared with the basic version was much greater than in the case of the 1943 TPV.

The TP21 (TerrängPersonvagn 21), which entered production in 1953, boasted considerably better terrain mobility than its predecessor a decade before. This was due mainly to three factors:

Firstly, the large wheels provided better grip and permitted a higher ground clearance. Secondly, differential locks on both axles ensured that the vehicle could be driven even when one pair of wheels was slipping. Thirdly, the shortened wheelbase afforded improved mobility and handling (the earlier TPV had been built on the same chassis as the original taxi version).

The body was shorter than the normal taxi body and differed from the basic version in appearance. In the case of the TP21, the designers opted for a completely flat roof, with an opening hatch for the aircraft spotter.

The TP21 became beloved of the Swedish Defence Forces (although no other army bought the relatively expensive model, despite Volvo's initiative of publishing a translated brochure).

An estate version was also developed in an attempt to interest 'civilian' customers in the TP21. However, the attractive model which resulted never reached the production stage.

No more big Volvo taxis were developed after the PV831/832. For this reason, future military terrain vehicles would be classified as trucks, with the exception of the 91 pre-production vehicles built prior to series production of the L3314. These bore the label 'P2304' in accordance with the model designations in use at the time, 'P' standing for 'car', '2' for 'estate', '3' for 'third planned version', '0' for 'petrol engine' and '4' for 'four-wheel drive'.*

* The first planned estate model (P210) was the updated Duett, while the second (P220) was the Amazon Combi.

Bottom left: Volvo TP21 terrain vehicle. Below: The P2304, which superseded the TP21. The other pictures on these pages show a PV830 series taxi.

Model	Period of manufacture	Number built	Wheelbase, cm	Track width (front/rear), cm	Swept volume, cm³	Engine rating, hp	No. of forward speeds
PV831–834	1950–58	6,216	325/355	151/152	3,670	90	3
TP21	1953–58	720	310	157/160	3,670	90	8
P2304	1959–61	91	210	132/134	1,583	60	8

The Duett – two for the price of one!

Although Volvo had produced estate models before (the earliest being the 1927/28 'Commercial Traveller'), it was the 1953 Volvo Duett which was the true forerunner of the hundreds of thousands of such cars that the company was later to build.

Since the start of production in 1927, it had always been possible to order a car without a body, whether to fit the chassis with attractive (and expensive!), custom-built coachwork, or to build a practical and less expensive van or light truck. Once production of the PV444 began to outstrip the demand, Volvo management decided to introduce a bare-chassis version of the model. Since the PV was equipped with a monocoque body, this version was provided with a light frame to take whatever body the customer chose to add. The designation of the new version was easily coined – the designers simply picked the next number after '444' and the model became known as the 445.

In 1949, the 445 was introduced in *Ratten* as a practical, small van powered by a 40-hp B4B engine and equipped with the same dashboard as the PV444 (with the instruments in the middle). Between then and the latter half of 1950, about 500 examples of this first version were produced as vans, estates and small pickup trucks.

The 445 chassis was also used by several bodybuilders to build a small number of very attractive cabriolets during the early years of the 1950s, although these were expensive at almost SKr20,000 and their days were numbered when the Volvo Sport was introduced. Perhaps more than any other Volvo model, these have now achieved cult status among enthusiasts.

An increasing number of 445-based vans and estate cars was produced by independent firms between 1949 and 1953, leading Volvo to consider the production of theses bodies itself. Apart from the obvious financial benefits, this promised an improvement in quality (something which varied

Overleaf: An attractive cabriolet built on a PV445 chassis.

among the many small independents). Intensive design work was initiated, culminating in the introduction of the Volvo PV445 Duett, a bodied van-cum-estate model which was delivered ex-works. Light truck versions (fitted with a cab and platform) were still produced by independent bodybuilders and were never referred to as 'Duetts'.

The Duetts of the 1950s were produced in several different versions. These included an estate van, an estate car (with more comfortable interior trim), a van with plain sides and a van without a rear seat, but with one or more windows to the rear of the front doors. None of these versions had rear side doors; all Duetts were 'three-door' vehicles (or 'four-door' if the rear, side-hinged doors were regarded as two).

The PV445 Duett quickly became a legend due to its almost unlimited load capacity, its easy-to-load cargo space and its tasteful lines (which were made even more elegant by an attractive two-tone finish).

Volvo had probably conceived the PV445 Duett primarily as a small van which could also be used as a private car in exceptional cases. However, the latter purpose soon took over, at least in the company's advertisements and literature. A Duett brochure of the 1950s contains illustrations portraying the model

1949–69

as a car for weekend and holiday use, showing a happy family enjoying the outdoor life, with a tent pitched close by, and adults and children bathing in the background.

The model remained basically unchanged throughout its production life. Like the PV544, however, it acquired a single-piece windscreen (although not until 1960) and was then rechristened the P210 Duett. In 1962 (about six months later than other car models), it was also equipped with the B18 engine and a 12-volt electrical system. The last Duett – a model which was loved to the end and was missed as few others – left the line in 1969.

Above and facing page: Volvo P210 Duett. Left: A toy model of the car by Somerville.

Model	Period of manufacture	Number built	Wheelbase, cm	Track width (front/rear), cm	Swept volume, cm³	Engine rating, hp	No. of forward speeds
PV445	1949–60	41,790	260	130/132	1,414–1,583	44–85	3
P210	1960–69	55,508	260	130/132	1,583–1,778	60–85	4

A plastic beauty – the Volvo Sport

Now owned by Gunnar Blomquist, a Gothenburg garage owner, this P1900 prototype chassis has survived to the present day.

Some Volvos have been loved. Others have become legends. But the P1900 has achieved almost mythical status.

The irony is that Volvo's most criticised car ever has also become its most admired – at least in hindsight.

Gunnar Engellau, who became head of Volvo in 1956, is famous as the man who initiated exports of the company's cars to the USA. However, this claim is not correct, although exports to North America did take off in earnest during his time at the helm.

It was actually Assar Gabrielsson who took this initiative towards the end of his tenure at the head of the company he had founded in 1926. Although the venture was afterwards portrayed as a gamble against all the odds, it was not. In the early 1950s, many European carmakers had taken the same step. Several, such as MG, Jaguar and Triumph, had been successful with their sports models while others, including Austin (with its Atlantic) and Sunbeam (with the first version of the Alpine), had failed.

The prospect of selling Volvos in large numbers in the USA was obviously a tempting one. And, given the success of the British, a sports car must have seemed the likeliest type of model to succeed.

So the design of the 'Volvo Sport' must have been on Gabrielsson's mind when he visited the USA in 1953 to enrol the assistance of Glasspar, a company which was experienced in the production of glass fibre-reinforced boats and car bodies. 'Plastic' bodies not only reduce kerb weight (ordinary sheet steel, aluminium and glass fibre-reinforced plastic have specific weights of 7.8, 2.7 and 1.5 g/cm^3 respectively), but require minimal investment in production tools. As a result, a series of successful European sports cars with glass fibre bodies saw the light of day in the middle and late 1950s. These included the Deutsch-Bonnet HBR5 from France and the Lotus Elite from Britain (the former with a central, tubular frame and the latter with a monocoque body).

Glass fibre-reinforced plastic has also been used as a body material in the USA. The most famous and

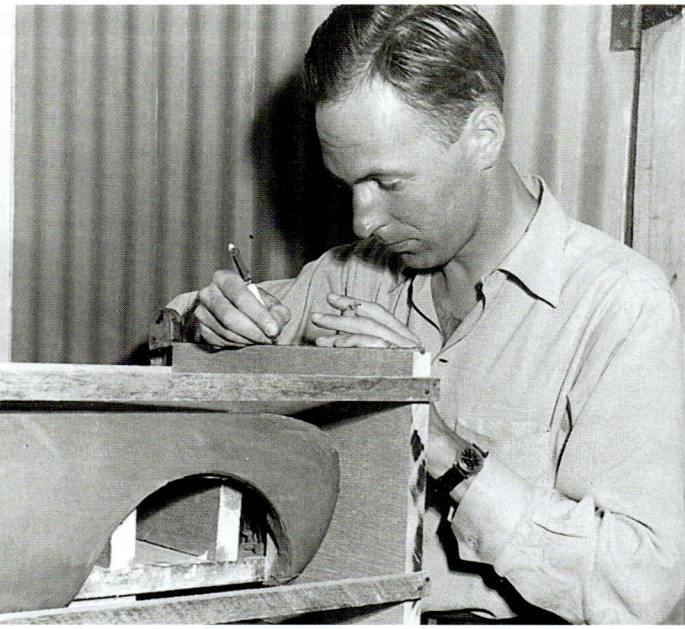

Below and bottom right: Development of the first model of the P1900 at the Glasspar plant in the USA.

1954-57

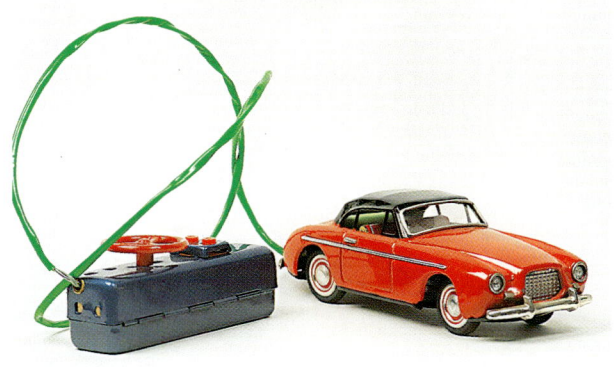

Left, far left and below: Pictures of the first series-built P1900 (chassis No. 01). Below, centre: A toy model from the 1950s, complete with electric drive and cable-operated steering.

most enduring example of the technology is the classic Chevrolet Corvette (1953-) which, with successive restyling, has been in production for five decades. Other 'plastic' sports cars from North America have included the Kaiser Darrin (1954-55), which was styled by Howard A. 'Dutch' Darrin, and the Studebaker Avanti (1963-64), the work of Raymond Loewy.

Glasspar was commissioned to build a prototype for evaluation by Volvo management, principally Gabrielsson. Gustaf Larson was no longer head of the design department, otherwise the model would almost certainly have had a steel body (which would have been better, but also much less exciting).

The Glasspar prototype received the green light and a small series of almost 70 cars was produced. Of these, about 50 have survived to the present day – a record number in this context.

The P1900 was similar to many of the models produced at the time by other small carmakers. The body was built on a tubular frame. The technical components, including a 'souped-up' 70-hp B4B engine (designated B14A) and a three-speed gearbox, were derived mainly from the PV444. The elegant interior trim featured special instrumentation and real leather upholstery.

However, the price was even higher than that of the handcrafted cabriolets built on the PV445 chassis and over twice that of a contemporary PV.

The P1900 was (and is) a beautiful car with high performance and excellent handling characteristics. It certainly deserved a better fate than to be 'killed off' by Gunnar Engellau after a well-publicised, long-distance test drive.

The PV444 and PV544 became particularly renowned for their performance in the USA, where they won many competitions. And, with its teething problems solved, the P1900 would certainly have given Volvo's exports to the USA the additional boost that Gabrielsson had hoped and planned.

However, it was not to be, although the go-ahead to develop the P1800 in a coupé version was given precisely as the P1900 received the thumbs-down. Today, the heritage of the P1900 lives on in the C70 Convertible, which is not only beautiful, but can travel almost 100 km/h faster than its illustrious predecessor!

Taken in 1956, the publicity photograph overleaf shows the first series-built version of the P1900.

Model	Period of manufacture	Number built	Wheelbase, cm	Track width (front/rear), cm	Swept volume, cm³	Engine rating, hp	No. of forward speeds
P1900	1954–57	67	240	130/132	1,414	70	3

– 53 –

Immortal two-tone beauty

The importance of the P120 Amazon to Volvo as an automaker can hardly be overstated. For the first time, the company was able to offer a safe, spacious, four-door family car powered by a modern and economical four-cylinder, OHV engine. The company was now targeting a much bigger group of car buyers (its earlier, relatively expensive large and medium-sized models had been the preserve of the better-off).

The new arrival was actually intended to be a considerably bigger car with a V8 engine, capable of competing on equal terms with the US models which were enjoying major popularity in Sweden at the time. Although a prototype known as the 'Philip' – which bore a strong resemblance to the American Kaiser Manhattan model and was powered by the V8 engine later to be used in Volvo's light trucks – was built, this relatively big car never reached the production stage.

The P120 (the 'Amazon' name was used only in some countries) was the first series-built model to be designed by the noted Volvo designer, Jan Wilsgaard, who had clearly been influenced by the trendsetting Italian styling of the 1950s. This was a new departure for Volvo since the company's earlier cars had generally been influenced by American styling.

The model was its most elegant in the two-tone finishes which were the only options available during the initial years of production in the late 1950s. Once the finish was changed to a single colour at the beginning of the 1960s, it lost a great deal of the

1956–70

elegance which Wilsgaard had created so successfully, inspired by Italian models and the colour schemes used on contemporary American four-door cars.

Under the skin, the Amazon was of conventional design. Despite its bigger format, the wheelbase was the same as in the PV444 (260 cm), although the track width had been increased and the body was wider. The extra doors were a welcome addition since they made it considerably easier for the rear-seat passengers to enter and leave the car. Compared with their counterparts in the PV444, rear-seat passengers in the Amazon enjoyed almost regal comfort. In addition, they now had side windows to wind down if they felt too enclosed.

In mechanical terms, the PV444 and the Amazon P120 were very similar. The B16 engine in the latter was basically a larger-bore version of the B4B used in the PV444. The first 60-hp unit was soon followed by an 85-hp 'Sport' version with twin SU carburettors (the same unit was installed shortly afterwards in the US version of the PV444L). The famous B18 engine was introduced in 1961, both in a 75-hp version (in the Amazon 121) and in a 90-hp twin-carburettor version (in the Amazon 122S Sport).

Despite its apparently limited horsepower

In its original two-tone finish, the P1200 Amazon was an extremely attractive car. Its character was often reinforced by accessories, such as cushions and extra badges.

(especially in comparison with the American V8s of the day), the P120 Amazon became known as a car which could leave most others standing. Among other reasons, this was due to the relatively large swept volume of the B18 relative to its size, combined with a robustness and standard of roadholding which few of the model's contemporaries could match.

The gearbox used initially was the same three-speed unit as in the PV444, although a four-speed option was soon added. Electrically operated overdrive, which gave the driver a choice of five speeds, became available as an extra at a later date. By the mid-1960s, the Amazon owner could even enjoy the luxury of an automatic transmission – complete with an 'Automatic' badge on the boot lid to impress the neighbours!

The Amazon became a legend mainly for its standard of safety, which was unsurpassed for the time. From the very first, attachments for two-point seat belts were standard. And from 1959 on, it became the first car in the world to be fitted with factory-fitted, three-point seat belts as standard equipment (as was the PV544).

The four-door version of the Amazon remained basically unchanged during its decade or so of manufacture. With the exception of the engine change (from the B16 to the B18), the upgrading of the electrical system from 6 to 12 volts (which was implemented at the same time) and the introduction of improved gearboxes, the P120 was a complete car from its introduction in 1956 to its replacement by the P144 in 1967.

Although more or less the same size, the PV444/544 and Amazon were fundamentally very different cars and were regarded as such buyers. Whereas the PV444/544 was seen as a small, economical model, the Amazon was regarded as the big car of everybody's dreams. Initially, however, the

The Amazon was very popular as a toy model (the one pictured below is by Spot-On).

Complemented by two-door and estate versions, the Amazon became a legend. Even today, it still serves as a utility vehicle.

Amazon was available only in a four-door version in a Sweden which – remarkably enough – had always preferred two-door models.

A two-door variant (P130) was added to the Amazon range at the beginning of the 1960s as the PV544 started to become obsolescent. Unlike today, when a two-door car is referred to as a 'coupé' and is considerably more expensive than its saloon equivalent, the P130 Amazon was presented as an economy variant of its four-door brother. However, it gradually assumed the position it deserved and became the only saloon version in the range in autumn 1967.

The Amazon Favorit was introduced to retain price-sensitive customers when the PV544 was discontinued. This version was recognised most easily by the rubber mouldings around the windows, and was available only in black or white. Technically, it was distinguished from other Amazons by its three-speed gearbox (the last time a unit of this type was used in a Volvo car). However, the status-conscious Swedes gave the Favorit a lukewarm reception and it was soon discontinued.

The most sporty Amazon of all (the GT) appeared in 1966 (as the 1967 model). Powered by the same engine as the P1800S sports car, this boasted twin spotlamps and more comprehensive instrumentation, with a rev counter as standard equipment.

Introduced in 1962, the third Amazon body was almost certainly intended to exploit the success achieved by the now-obsolescent Duett.

The Amazon P220 Combi was an elegant car with a divided tailgate (in the American style) and different rear doors from the P120 and P130 saloons. It soon gained acceptance as an exclusive alternative to the P210 Duett, although it never displaced the latter as a utility vehicle (whether due to its higher price or the Duett's superb durability).

The Amazon Combi (the model was not referred to as an estate) played a major role in Volvo's history as the first exemplar of the exclusive character possessed by all Volvo estates since then.

Model	Period of manufacture	Number built	Wheelbase, cm	Track width (front/rear), cm	Swept volume, cm^3	Engine rating, hp	No. of forward speeds
P120	1956–67	234,208	260	132	1,583–1,778	60–95	3–5 (A)
P130	1961–70	359,918	260	132	1,778–1,986	75–118	3–5 (A)
P220	1962–69	73,197	260	132	1,778–1,986	75–100	4–5 (A)

Refinement

Facing page, bottom left: The PV544 was extremely popular as a model car. One of the best examples was made by Brooklin.

Below: Design work on the new PV544 was completed in 1956-57.

In their famous 1936 sales manual, Assar Gabrielsson and Gustaf Larson wrote that "Volvo does not make changes for their own sake". This quotation was particularly appropriate to the PV544. Although described as 'new' on its introduction in 1958, it was really 'just' a revamped version of its popular and reliable predecessor, the PV444L.

The changes were nonetheless welcome. The big, single-piece windscreen afforded better visibility, as did the generously sized rear window. The interior was more attractive compared with the 444, while the top of the dashboard was padded for safety. The effective width of the rear seat was increased by the folding design of the armrest, enabling three passengers to travel 'legally' in the rear.

Now, Swedish motorists could finally buy a fast PV 'Sport' with an 85-hp engine (with its popular and characteristic noise), a choice of three or four-speed gearboxes, and the option of a standard or

special version. (The range of combinations was, however, limited; Volvo was no longer the tiny carmaker of earlier years which could build cars almost to individual customer specifications.)

With the exception of the windscreen and rear window, the new model was generally similar in appearance to the PV444L, although the golden 'V' on the grille and on the boot lid had disappeared. The styling was subsequently to remain more or less unchanged until the model reached the end of its successful history in 1965.

Volvo's strategy proved successful. In its seven years of production from 1958 to 1965, the PV544 was produced in significantly greater numbers than the PV444 (1944-58).

The modifications became fewer as the years went on, although compared with the almost-identical PV544A and PV544B, the PV544C was a much-improved (and faster) car with its brand-new B18 engine, five-speed gearbox and 12 V electrics. However, the changes to the 'D', 'E', 'F' and 'G' models were cosmetic; for example, new types of hub caps were among the most important 'innovations' in 1962 and 1964. For a brief period in autumn 1965, the PV544 Sport was equipped with the more powerful 95-hp engine used in the 1966 Amazon Sport, making the 1966 PV544G

1958–65

the fastest of all production versions of the PV444/PV544 series.

The PV544 became a legendary rally car (at least in later years). Both Gunnar Anderson (1963) and Tom Trana (1964) became European rally champions in the model, while Evy Rosqvist and Sylvia Österberg won the European ladies' title in 1959 and 1963 respectively.

Today, thanks to its excellent handling and superb durability, the PV544 Sport is a popular choice among motoring enthusiasts competing in classic car rallies. And the model is still to be seen in everyday use on Swedish roads, both in summer and winter – impressive for a car last produced over thirty years ago and first unveiled almost twenty years prior to that.

Below: The last PV544s were handed over to their owners at a ceremony held at Volvo's Gothenburg plant.

Model	Period of manufacture	Number built	Wheelbase, cm	Track width (front/rear), cm	Swept volume, cm³	Engine rating, hp	No. of forward speeds
PV544	1958–65	243,996	260	128/130	1,583–1,778	60–95	4

Most beautiful Volvo ever?

The early P1800s built by Jensen in Britain were recognisable by an attractive badge on the post between the rear side window and rear window.

Take a Swedish sports car. With a body styled in Italy by Frua and produced in Scotland. Assembled in England. And sold mainly in the USA. If ever a Volvo had an international history, it was surely the P1800.

The P1800 was to become famous as the car driven by Roger Moore in *The Saint*, the TV series based on the detective novels of Leslie Charteris. However, it deserves to be remembered as more than just the 'star' of a TV series; it had (and has) its own distinctive qualities.

As a sports car, the P1800 achieved a level of success that the P1900 (which was perhaps more spectacular) never quite reached. The reasons were many. One was the model's attractive styling, another its robust construction, which was very similar to that of the PV544 and Amazon. A third reason (proclaimed by Volvo in its US advertising) was that the P1800, although more expensive than many ordinary cars, was only a fraction of the price of a 'real' sports car like a Ferrari – but still came with elegant Italian lines.

The P1800 project was initiated when the P1900 received the *coup de grâce* from Gunnar Engellau in 1957. The project was effectively led by the legendary Helmer Pettersson (who had been involved in the design of the PV444 during the war years). His son, Pelle Pettersson (later to become a famed boat designer), was then working for Frua in Italy and provided a vital link which eliminated many of the cultural clashes normally associated with joint ventures between two peoples. The progress of the design work was greatly assisted by Helmer Pettersson's frequent visits to Italy (Pettersson loved to drive and appears to have spent many hours on the fast German autobahns on his journeys to and fro).

Below: Early Swedish-built examples of the P1800 differed very little from the first version.

1800E.

It was decided, from the outset, that the P1800 would be based on Amazon components, guaranteeing maximum reliability and advanced handling characteristics (the Amazon itself proved to be a top-class rally car).

From the very beginning, it was clear that the model would be equipped with a more powerful version of the B18 engine (initially with a 100-hp rating, and increasing successively to 108 and 115 hp). This was not used in any other car (except the Amazon 123GT, a 'special' which was available with the 115-hp version under the bonnet from 1966 on). The B18 engine in the P1800 received the designation 'B' to distinguish it from the 'A' (the standard, single-carburettor version) and the 'D' (the 'ordinary' Sport version used in the PV544 Sport and Amazon Sport). The 'missing' letter 'C' was used for a downrated version used in the Volvo Buster Bensin tractor.

A few prototypes of the P1800 were completed in 1959 and the model entered production in 1961. Since Volvo did not have sufficient production capacity to build the car itself during the introductory phase, it was assembled for a time by sports car manufacturer Jensen in Britain (which was also producing the Austin Healey 3000 for the BMC Group at the time).

The quality of the British-built cars proved unsatisfactory and production was transferred to Gothenburg after a couple of years (Volvo was obliged to negotiate a settlement with Jensen to terminate the venture). Somewhat later, the model designation was changed to P1800S and the engine rating was increased to 108 hp. The Jensen assembly shop in which the P1800 had been built was later used to produce the Sunbeam Tiger sports car, a version of the Sunbeam Alpine powered by a Ford V8 engine.

The P1800 proved popular and only some details were modified in the decade or so of its

Overleaf: HRH Crown Prince Carl Gustaf (now HM Carl XVI Gustaf) with a Volvo 1800 ES.

A model P1800S by Dinky Toys.

Below: Volvo P1800S.

production. In terms of styling, the most significant changes were made in 1964, when the characteristic upturned 'overriders' on the front bumper were eliminated, and in 1966, when the curved side trim, which had previously terminated immediately behind the door, was 'straightened' and extended further towards the rear of the car. The grille was modified in 1964 and 1969.

The model became increasingly powerful as time went on. The original 100-hp version had been

extremely fast for its day – and became even livelier with the introduction of the 118-hp B20 engine in 1968. However, perhaps the most sought-after version of all was the 1800E (the last variant), which was powered by a 135-hp fuel-injection engine. In all cases, the gearbox was the same as that used in the Amazon/140 series, usually a four-speed manual unit with electrically operated overdrive (initially, the same box was available without overdrive at a slightly lower price). Automatic transmission was introduced in time and became particularly common in North America, to which a growing proportion of the cars was exported.

Several variants were added to the basic 2+2-seat version. Cabriolet versions were built both in the USA (on the initiative of 'Volvoville', the Volvo dealer, which also boasted that its model had an additional 15 cm of headroom in the rear) and in Britain (by Crayford, then an extremely progressive company which specialised in converting saloon cars to drophead coupés in small series).

Zagato of Italy built a fastback concept, presumably to tempt Volvo to include it in its standard range. This did not come to fruition, however, and Coggiola, another Italian stylist, instead designed a modified rear end which transformed the 1800E into a sporty and exclusive estate (the 1800ES). Unfortunately, this version was produced only for two years, the first year in parallel with the 1800E and the second as the sole heir of the P1800 introduced at the end of the 1950s.

The 1800ES, in particular, became a cult model, perhaps unfairly to the first version. The original 1960s version of the P1800 was an underestimated car with attractive Italian lines, excellent handling characteristics and mechanical equipment which might best be described as indestructible. It boasted an extremely high standard of comfort, although its higher weight compared with the PV544 and its lower body (which reduced the driver's visibility) made it less suitable for 'serious' classic rallying.

The pictures on these pages show several examples of the 1800ES

Model	Period of manufacture	Number built	Wheelbase, cm	Track width (front/rear), cm	Swept volume, cm^3	Engine rating, hp	No. of forward speeds
P1800/1800	1959–72	34,907	245	132	1,778–1,986	100–135	4–5 (A)
1800ES	1971–73	8,077	245	132	1,986	107–135	5 (A)

Safety and prestige

Far right: An early version of the Volvo 144.

Whereas the PV444 (and even earlier Volvo cars) looked liked 'miniature' American models, the Amazon and P1800 were inspired by Italian styling in many respects. In 1966, Volvo found its own styling language – characterised by austere lines and a third side window – which was to set the tone for the coming decades and create a 'Volvo' image.

Introduced in 1966, the 140 series was a logical successor to the four-door Amazon as a safe family car with high performance and a robust character which ensured unprecedented long life.

Under the skin, the four-door version (144) launched in 1966 was equipped with more or less the same engine and gearbox options as the Amazon. These took the form of a B18 engine (rated at either 75 or 95 hp) and the choice of a four-speed manual gearbox (with or without overdrive) or automatic transmission. In 1968, the famed B18 was replaced by the larger-bore B20 unit, providing brisker acceleration (although the top speed was only marginally higher).

Below: Volvo 142.

The exemplary safety of the Volvo 144 earned it numerous awards. Most remarkable was the new braking system, which featured disc brakes all round (a feature then found only on high-performance cars and, remarkably enough, also on the little, rear-engined Renault 8). This was not the only unusual feature of the system; even more unique were the dual braking circuits, each of which served both front wheels and one rear wheel. This configuration ensured that almost full braking power was applied and that directional stability was maintained even if one of the circuits failed.

The design of the body as a protective 'cage' also contributed to the model's exceptional safety. Although the crumple zone concept is now accepted design practice, it was so unusual at the time that many 'experts' were sceptical of it, believing that a car should remain intact in an accident (and forgetting that the occupants could easily be killed by the severe g-forces!).

Like all Volvo's, 140 series models were superb

1966-75

The Volvo 145 was modified successively as seen in these pictures. Note the altered grille and rear window styling.

winter cars, thanks to their big wheels and substantial weight, which ensured that the drive wheels were adequately loaded under all conditions.

On this occasion, Volvo was quicker to introduce a cheaper, two-door version of the model, the 142, as a complement to the four-door 144. Even so, it continued to produce the even cheaper (and now elderly) two-door Amazon right up to 1970, to ensure that less affluent customers did not abandon the marque.

Added in 1968, the 145 estate soon became popular, both in the standard and 'Express' versions. With its raised roof, the latter was particularly favoured by newspaper dispatchers, who not only had to get their papers on the stands as quickly as possible, but also had to ensure the comfort and safety of their drivers (many of whom were just a little inclined to drive on the wrong side of the speed limits…).

The first estate was unusual for the two side windows behind each rear door (one of these windows could be opened to improve the interior air circulation). However, the designers reverted to a more conventional configuration featuring a single, long window on the 1971 model.

The 140 series underwent little change during its period of production from 1966 to 1974, due mainly to legal requirements in other countries. American legislation was the main influence in this context by contributing, for example, to the development of the increasingly heavier (and uglier) bumpers designed to protect the car from damage in low-speed impacts.

Neither was the two-door 140 built exclusively as a 'budget' model. Like its predecessors, the PV544 Sport and Amazon 123GT, it was available in a deluxe, two-door version (142GT) with the powerful 135-hp, fuel-injection engine from the 1800E sports car. Produced for barely a year, this is regarded as one of the best Volvos ever by enthusiasts.

The 144 acquired a remarkable sibling in 1968

Far left: A later version of the Volvo 144.

Production of the Volvo 164.

The original version of the Volvo 164 (below) and a later version (facing page).

in the shape of the 164. Powered by a six-cylinder version of the B20 engine, this possessed superb reserves of speed, making it an extremely comfortable touring car (but hardly 'sporty' due to its weight). Although based on the same body as the 144, the new model had an elongated front reminiscent of the P1900 sports car of 1956.

Powered initially by a 130-hp carburettor engine, the 164 possessed speed resources which were much more than 'adequate'. The performance (and the already high fuel consumption!) was boosted even further by the introduction of a fuel-injection version of this unit developing no less than 175 hp.

The Volvo 164 was manufactured until 1975, a year more than the 140 series, and was the first six-cylinder Volvo to appear since the PV831/832 taxis were discontinued in 1957. It was to be followed by a long, unbroken series of luxurious, high-performance, six-cylinder models from the Volvo 264, 760 and 960/S90 to the present-day S80 which, therefore, is its direct, linear descendant.

Model	Period of manufacture	Number built	Wheelbase, cm	Track width (front/rear), cm	Swept volume, cm^3	Engine rating, hp	No. of forward speeds
144	1966–74	523,808	260/262	135/133	1,778–1,986	85–135	4–5 (A)
142	1967–74	413,006	260/262	135/139	1,778–1,986	85–135	4–5 (A)
145	1967–74	268,327	260/262	135/139	1,778–1,986	85–135	4–5 (A)
164	1968–75	146,008	270/272	135/139	2,978	145–175	4–5 (A)

'Safety first'

The introduction of the three-point seat belt at the end of the 1950s, together with the Volvo 144's revolutionary safety body and braking system, propelled the company towards a position of leadership in the automotive safety field. However, it was really the VESC (Volvo Experimental Safety Car) which established Volvo, not simply as one of the safest makes of car in the world, but as the leader in the field.

The VESC actually started life, not 'just' as a concept car, but as the first of a whole new generation of Volvos intended to replace the 140/160 series in the mid-1970s. In the event, the energy crisis intervened and put an end to the development of the B35 V8 engine which was to be used in the most powerful version. Thus, in autumn 1974, P.G. Gyllenhammar, the recently appointed head of Volvo, committed the company to the development of a fundamentally refined and improved 140/160 series, under the designations '240' and '260'.

In the light of its role as a major exporter of cars to the USA, and of the safety debate which was raging there at the time, it was decided to build a small series of experimental cars with the focus on safety. Other aspects would not be permitted to inhibit total concentration on the development of a safe concept car, which would help the company's engineers to design safer Volvo cars and would generate some well-needed PR for the company.

From its appearance, the VESC might easily have been mistaken for nothing more than an early

1972

244. Nothing could be further from the truth, although its front-end design did influence the 240/260 series, especially in terms of ensuring the integrity of the crumple zone in a head-on collision.

The VESC was necessarily a fairly heavy car due to its extremely strong body, with its integral safety cage and 'spring-loaded' front bumper, which could withstand a collision at 10 mph without damage. Nevertheless, its design was to contribute to the development of new generations of safe Volvo cars which, although lighter, would be superior to their 'parent' in terms of crash safety.

The model was equipped with ABS brakes to further improve its active safety.

The interior trim was a model from the aspect of passive safety. Every surface with which the driver could conceivably collide in an accident was provided with soft padding. To ensure 100% seat

belt usage (given that by no means all motorists were convinced of their effectiveness and that others simply ignored them), the belts were applied automatically, without action by the occupant. The provision of front and rear-seat airbags was yet another innovation which was eventually to find its way into standard production cars.

In other respects, the VESC boasted numerous, more or less practical innovations, such as a TV camera instead of a conventional rear-view mirror.

The various VESCs were finished in spectacular colours, including a striking flame yellow similar to the one of the finishes later available in the 240 series. There were several reasons, one being that 'loud' colours helped to produce better films and photographs of the various crash tests. In addition, however, the Volvo engineers almost certainly considered the potential contribution of such colours to traffic safety, surmising that the number of traffic accidents might be reduced by encouraging buyers to choose a particular finish not only for its aesthetic appeal, but also for its visibility to other road users.

More than any other car, the VESC made Volvo a leader in international automotive research. Most of the prototypes were used for safety studies and were destroyed in various tests; however, a couple of examples have been preserved for posterity and are now on view in the Volvo Museum in Gothenburg.

Dutch town car

An interior view of the Volvo 66.

Having taken over the reins at Volvo at the beginning of the 1970s (some years before the energy crisis), the legendary Pehr G. Gyllenhammar was quick to realise that Volvo again needed a 'small' car. Since there was almost no possibility of developing such a model in a short time – especially since all of the components used in the existing Volvo range were designed for medium-sized cars – the only solution was to acquire a small manufacturer specialising in such vehicles.

Attention soon turned to van Doorne's Personenautofabriek DAF BV in Eindhoven, Holland, and Volvo bought 33% of its shares at the end of 1972. Although ingenious and revolutionary, Hubert Jozef van Doorne's steplessly variable, automatic transmission was then regarded with some scepticism; today, long after its abandonment by DAF/Volvo, the concept is still being used successfully in several makes of car.

To understand why P.G. Gyllenhammar set his sights on DAF, it is necessary to consider the company's fifteen-year history as an independent automaker. This coincided with a decade and a half of exciting automotive development, at a time when the devastation of the war years was beginning to recede and the peoples of central Europe were to be 'given wheels'. Sadly, it is sometimes forgotten today that DAF was a highly progressive carmaker under the dynamic leadership of the van Doorne brothers.

Their revolutionary small car, the DAF 600, had been launched with automatic transmission as standard as far back as 1958. This was followed, in 1962, by the more powerful DAF 750 and by the 'deluxe' Daffodil (an obvious play on the company name).

A larger model (DAF 44) styled by Michelotti of Italy was introduced in 1967. This was still powered by DAF's own two-cylinder, air-cooled, four-stroke, opposed-piston engine.

Performance was improved considerably when the DAF 55, with the same body as the 44 and a four-cylinder Renault engine under the hood, was introduced in 1968.

Although basically the same car as the DAF 55,

1975-80

the DAF 66 (1973) was equipped with a highly advanced rear suspension of the de Dion type (representing the birth of the DAF's extraordinary roadholding qualities). The 66 was also produced in a cabriolet version, but only for the Dutch armed forces.

The model's roadholding was to earn it prestigious class victories in rally events. Neither was DAF a stranger to the racing circuit; in 1965, the company had developed a single-seat Formula Junior car with a Variomatic transmission.

Following Volvo's acquisition of a minority shareholding in DAF, Volvo dealers began to market DAF and Volvo models in parallel to a limited extent.

In 1975, Volvo expanded its interest to take a majority shareholding in the Dutch company and van Doorne´s Personenautofabriek DAF BV became Volvo Car BV. Volvo had acquired the opportunity of building another 'people's car'.

The DAF cars continued to be sold under their original name for the first few years. The exception was the biggest of the models, the DAF 66, which was renamed the Volvo 66 in autumn 1975. This was available in both saloon and estate versions.

Relatively successful, the Volvo 66 became accepted as the 'baby' of the Volvo range. It was to remain part of the range until 1980 (by then only in a two-door version, the estate having been discontinued in 1978). However, apart from acquiring a small car, Volvo had other reasons for buying DAF; the Dutch were also developing a medium-sized model (the DAF 77/Volvo 343) which would fit neatly into the company's range.

The Volvo 66 saloon (above) and Volvo 66 estate (left).

Model	Period of manufacture	Number built	Wheelbase, cm	Track width (front/rear), cm	Swept volume, cm³	Engine rating, hp	No. of forward speeds
Volvo 66 saloon	1975-80	77,637	226	131/124	1,108-1,289	47-57	A
Volvo 66 estate	1975-78	28,500	226	131/124	1,108-1,289	47-57	A

Enduring legend

This page: Volvo 244.

The 140/160 series (with the exception of the 164, which was produced for a further year for a number of markets) were succeeded by the 240/260 in 1974. At the time, Volvo management hoped that the revitalised new series would still be modern a year or so into the 1980s. Little did they suspect that a legend had been born.

The 240 (which was by far the most popular and best-selling model of the 200 series throughout its life) was based on the final version of the 140. This was clear from the fact that the entire upper body and doors were identical to the latter, down to the recessed door handles and absence of front quarter-lights.

Otherwise, the 240/260 were completely new cars. The very first basic version (240L) was, admittedly, still equipped with the B20 engine; however, two completely new light-alloy engine families with overhead camshafts – the B21 for the 240 and the B27 for the 260 – had been developed to comply with emission control regulations and to reduce the fuel consumption.

The new B21 engine was available in both carburettor and fuel-injection versions. Used in the 240GL, the latter developed an impressive 140 hp (before the rating was reduced to meet emission control limits). The unit was popular with motorists for the speed it gave the car, for its smooth running and for its relatively modest fuel consumption (at least in comparison with the less lively and, above all, thirstier carburettor version). The B19, a variant of the B21 with a slightly lower swept volume, was introduced about a year later as a replacement for the reliable, but ageing B20, completing the transition from the 100 to the 200 series.

While the 240 was successfully replacing the 140, the 264 was superseding the 164. Under the bonnet, the 264 was equipped with a new V6 engine (B27) developed jointly by Volvo (for the 264), Renault (for the Renault 30 and Alpine A310 sports car) and Peugeot (for the Peugeot 604 and Talbot Tagora). Known as the 'PRV' (the initials stood for the three manufacturers), this unit had been conceived originally as a V8, but that proposal had been shelved because of the energy crisis. The B27 was also available in carburettor and fuel-injection versions. However, since the first of these (which was intended as an 'economy' version) was not

1974-93

comparable even to the injection B21 in terms of performance, and since it also had a much higher fuel consumption, it was soon discontinued. Never a success, the PRV was a factor in the failure of the 264 to raise Volvo's status to that of a maker of prestigious and luxurious cars (for the time being at least).

The four-door 244 and 264, the 245 estate and the two-door 242 were introduced initially in autumn 1974 (for the first time, Volvo was able to launch all three versions concurrently since the bodies were already available from the 140 series). Two further versions – the more luxurious 265 estate and the two-door 262 (which was sold only in North America) – were added in 1975. A further addition was the luxurious 264TE (Top Executive) VIP model (the suffix had been used before on a small series of lavishly equipped 164Es).

From the outset, the 240/260 series won a high reputation for its ruggedness, although it suffered initially from corrosion problems as a result of new environmental standards imposed on production plants at that time, requiring the introduction of different paints and the adoption of new painting methods. Although many carmakers experienced similar problems between 1974 and 1978 (all purchased their paints from a small number of independent, international suppliers), Volvo's problems were aggravated by the extensive use of salt on winter roads in Sweden. Nevertheless, the company met its obligations and many 240/260s were repainted free of charge to their owners.

Volvo celebrated its 50th anniversary in 1977. The occasion was marked by the launch of a 'sporty'

Above and left: Volvo 245.

Below: Its catalytic converter and oxygen sensor (Lambdasond) made the Volvo 240 one of the world's most environmentally compatible cars.

Far right: Volvo 262 Coupé.

coupé (262C) styled by Volvo itself and built from Swedish-made pressings, but assembled in Italy by Bertone (which was already building the 264TE limousine). A luxurious and well-equipped car, the new model was built only in limited numbers at a price which was high for the time. Available initially only in one colour (metallic silver) and with an imitation leather roof covering, the 262C eventually became available in other finishes (without the roof covering), including metallic yellow and metallic mid-blue, as well as black. Although it never became a best-seller, the 262C did reinforce Volvo's image as a maker of upmarket models, especially in North America.

An early forerunner of the C70 Coupé, the 262C was to be followed in the 1980s by the 780, which was also the work of Bertone. Its failure to make a real impact was partly due to a couple of inherent weaknesses, including the sluggishness of the B27 engine and the lack of headroom, which was low even for drivers of average height.

The styling of the 240 series was by no means cast in bronze. On the contrary, the initially anonymous front acquired greater character as time went on. Modifications to this effect included the introduction of square headlamps in 1978 followed, later still, by rectangular units. In 1979, the rear end, which was basically the same as on the 144, was modified to produce a more attractive, rounded shape. The boot threshold was lowered at the same time, easing the strain on the back when loading and unloading luggage.

An exclusive, sporty variant of the 242 was unveiled in 1978 (a step analogous to the introduction of its precursors, the PV544 Sport, 123GT and 142GL). The first version was powered by the B21E engine, which was replaced after a year by the bigger B23E (a variant first used in a special 244GLT model built for driving on the German autobahns). All 242GTs were finished in metallic silver with 'speed stripes' and came with super-exclusive interior trim featuring black seats with an orange stripe.

Volvo 264.

Soon afterwards, the B23E engine was also used in a four-door version (244GLT), which was produced for a greater number of markets. This was perhaps the version which was most appreciated by enthusiastic drivers (especially before the rating was reduced to comply with emission control standards in the 1980s).

The 244GLT with the B23 engine was recognisable by its silver-coloured 'GLT' badge. In an attempt to increase sales of the moderately popular B27E/B28E engines used in the 264, the 244GLT was also marketed with these as options at a modest extra premium. This 'budget 264' bore a golden badge.

Equipped with a six-cylinder Volkswagen engine, the diesel version of the 240 introduced at the end of 1979 was the direct opposite of the powerful GLTs (a five-cylinder version was also available for certain markets in which units over 2 litres were subject to punitive taxation).

The model was designed mainly to win back taxi owners to Volvo and was fairly successful in this respect as Volvos again became a familiar sight at Swedish taxi ranks for the first time in two decades. However, although it was an economical and comfortable vehicle for long-distance travel at average cruising speeds, it was a flop with 'ordinary' drivers.

The 760/740 series was introduced in succession to the 240/260 between 1982 and 1984. Although production of the 260 came to an end on schedule, the extraordinary popularity of the 240 (particularly the 245 estate version) contributed to its survival for almost a decade longer than planned. Towards the

Volvo 264 TE (Top Executive).

Volvo 262.

end of its life, the 245 (now known simply as the '240') was to achieve cult status in several countries, such as Italy and Britain, where it became a status symbol at the golf club and the theatre!

However, the series finally came to the end of the road in 1993, when the very last 245 left the line to occupy a place of honour in the Volvo Museum in Gothenburg.

Was the Volvo 240 the perfect family car? The answer must be 'yes'. But it was more than that. The model also achieved success in competition, both as a rallycross car and as the winning entrant in the 1985 European Touring Car Championship, in which it was driven by Thomas Lindström and Gianfranco Brancatelli. Although it must be admitted that their 242 developed 330 hp and reached a top speed of at least 260 km/h!

The Volvos 200 series was more than a safe, comfortable, functional and (in some versions) fast car. It was also an outstanding example of Volvo's leadership in environmental care, as exemplified by the introduction of its catalytic converter (with an oxygen sensor, or 'Lambdasond') in 1977. This advance was a landmark in the purification of exhaust gases as an environmental protection measure. Unfortunately, since the catalytic converter required the use of unleaded petrol, it could be used only in North America. Apathy on the part of the oil companies prevented widespread use of this revolutionary device throughout the world at large and the environment was to suffer accordingly for several years more.

Model	Period of manufacture	Number built	Wheelbase, cm	Track width (front/rear), cm	Swept volume, cm^3	Engine rating, hp	No. of forward speeds
242/240	1974–84	242,621	264	142/135	1,986–2,315	82–140	4–5 (A)
244/240	1974–93	1,483,399	264	142/135	1,784–2,849	68–155	4–5 (A)
245/240	1974–93	959,151	264	142/135	1,784–2,849	68–155	4–5 (A)
264/260	1974–82	132,390	264	142/135	2,664–2,849	121–155	5 (A)
262	1975–77	3,329	264	142/135	2,664–2,849	121–125	5 (A)
265/260	1975–85	35,061	264	142/135	2,664–2,849	121–156	5 (A)
262C	1977–81	6,622	264	142/135	2,664–2,849	129–155	5 (A)

'The Flying Dutchman'

Far right: The four-door version of the Volvo 340/360 was the choice of many owners who preferred a saloon.

The Volvo 343 was a practical family car with an easy-to-load luggage compartment.

Probably no Volvo was as underestimated as the 340/360 series, which was introduced in autumn 1976. Conceived originally by van Doornes Personenautofabriek BV as the DAF 77, it was rebadged as a Volvo following the takeover of the Dutch company.

Developed over a fifteen-year period, the 340/360 fulfilled many roles – including town car, small tourer, rallycross car and world record beater!

The 343 appeared in autumn 1976. Here, at last, was another 'small' Volvo, which would take over the 'people's Volvo' mantle last worn by the PV444/PV544, now out of production for just a decade. With the exception of the little DAF-designed Volvo 66, all of the models in the Volvo range had become relatively big and heavy due to their safe construction. As a result, the company needed a small car in the class which dominated – and continues to dominate – the continental European market.

Unfortunately, the first efforts were catastrophic. In the haste to develop the car, the design work was rushed and the detailed design was found to be poor when the model was introduced. Although not serious in technical terms, the shortcomings, such as defects in the interior trim, were numerous.

Once the initial problems had been solved, however, the 340/360 gained a loyal public. Over a million examples were built, making it one of the most popular Volvo series ever.

Technically, the 340/360 was conservative and exciting at the same time. Like all Volvo cars of the period, it was naturally rear-wheel driven. However, its favourable weight distribution gave it exceptional handling qualities, due primarily to the advanced de Dion-type rear suspension.

Picking a model from the 340 range was easy at

– 80 –

1976–91

first; there was only one choice – a three-door model with fully automatic Variomatic transmission (which eliminated the need for gearchanging) and with a modestly rated, 70-hp, 1.4-litre Renault engine under the hood. The range of bodies, engines and gearboxes increased as time went on.

A five-door version appeared in 1979. This was accompanied by an alternative to the Variomatic transmission in the form of a manual Volvo gearbox attached directly to the rear axle.

Performance was improved significantly with the introduction of the 343/345 DLS, which was powered by a 2-litre Volvo engine. In the first year, the presence of the new unit was advertised by a 'bump' on the bonnet; however, the front was later restyled, making it the same regardless of engine and harmonising it more closely with other models in the Volvo range. The 343/345 DLS was equipped initially with a carburettor engine. However, a fuel-injection unit and a more rigid body were introduced later, creating what was to be one of the best 'on-road' cars ever produced by Volvo. The model in question was the 360 GLT, which was blessed with perfect weight distribution, excellent roadholding and high performance.

A four-door saloon was added in 1984, followed by a more sedate diesel the next model year.

The 340 made its presence felt as a competition model. In 1980, Per-Inge Walfridsson defeated strong opposition to become European rallycross champion in the car, thanks to its superb handling and a newly developed 16-valve competition engine based on the B21. And Carl-Magnus Skogh, the legendary rally driver, piloted a plastic-bodied 343 to a world speed record for diesel cars up to 2 litres at Landvetter Airport, outside Gothenburg.

The 340 series won no beauty competitions. Despite (or, perhaps, because of) its unique looks, Bertone, the noted Italian bodybuilding firm, designed its own version of the 343 called the 'Tundra' which, unfortunately, never entered series production.

Volvo 345.

Model	Period of manufacture	Number built	Wheelbase, cm	Track width (front/rear), cm	Swept volume, cm^3	Engine rating, hp	No. of forward speeds
343/340/360	1976–90	505,969	240	135/138	1,397–1,986	55–115	5 (A)
345/340/360	1979–91	434,266	240	135/138	1,397–1,986	55–115	5 (A)
340/360 (4-d)	1983–89	146,171	240	135/138	1,397–1,986	55–115	5 (A)

The taxi as fine art

The 480 is often said to have been Volvo's first front-wheel drive car. Although this claim does contain a grain of truth, it is strictly incorrect. In fact, the company's first car of this type was built in 1976 as a working prototype (or design proposal) for a new generation of taxis, in a competition held by the world-famous Museum of Modern Art in New York.

Volvo's 'experimental taxi' was a working model which was optimised in terms of safety, function and ergonomics. Although resembling an estate car with its truncated rear end, it was actually a saloon. The styling was clearly influenced by the familiar London taxi, but was much more modern in spirit.

To minimise fuel consumption while producing acceptably clean exhaust gases, the vehicle was equipped with a six-cylinder, precombustion-chamber diesel engine designed for Volvo by the British firm of Ricardo. The choice of a fuel-efficient diesel was dictated by the latest energy crisis, which had given the industrialised nations a sharp reminder that world oil consumption would have to be reduced at any cost, and that maximum independence from the oil-producing OPEC nations would be essential in the future. As a taxi designed for the North American market, the model was equipped with automatic transmission.

Although relatively short, the car was very wide and fairly high, affording generous interior space, while the low floor facilitated entry, even for wheelchair-bound passengers. The floor itself was slightly convex and outward-sloping, making daily cleaning easier.

Apart from functionality and ergonomics, safety was the most striking characteristic of this unique vehicle. To simulate seat belt usage (never a strong point among taxi passengers), the rear was equipped with a padded safety 'boom', which was lowered in front of the occupants and also served as a comfortable armrest.

The driver was, of course, protected by a conventional, three-point seat belt. Being a taxi, however, the safety concept was interpreted more widely than usual. Thus, the driver was seated in a separate compartment provided with bulletproof glass and a special fare payment hatch as protection against potentially violent or criminal passengers.

Climate comfort was assured by air conditioning,

1976

with a roof-mounted intake to ensure that the inlet air was as pure as possible.

In addition to the short taxi version, Volvo pointed out that the same vehicle could easily be built (on a longer wheelbase) as a minibus or ambulance.

Although the competition attracted some interest in the USA, it had never been intended to create vehicles for mass production. Its real purpose was to improve taxi design in the short term and, with an eye to the future, to demonstrate that the taxi has the potential to make life easier for urban dwellers when cars are not essential.

As a front-wheel drive model, Volvo's experimental taxi remained a 'one-off' until a series-built car of this type appeared nine years later.

Electric 'mini-Volvo'

Together with safety, environmental care has always been one of Volvo's core values. This has been especially true since the major UN environmental conference held in Stockholm in 1972, at which the company, under the dynamic Pehr G. Gyllenhammar, played a leading and inspirational role.

In the latter half of the 1970s, Volvo introduced the revolutionary catalytic converter and oxygen sensor (Lambdasond), which purified petrol engine exhaust gases to an unprecendented extent. However, the company was also anxious to demonstrate that it was no stranger to the electric motor as a motive power source. The main advantage of an electric car is

the complete absence of emissions (although generation of the electricity used to recharge the vehicle batteries does have an environmental impact).

The main disadvantage of the electric car is associated, not with the vehicle itself or with the drive motor, but with the capacity of the on-board batteries. Although practically no research had been devoted to this aspect during the previous decade, Volvo chose to embody its ideas in the form of an electric town car, two prototypes of which were unveiled in autumn 1976.

1976

These pages: The two electric cars built by Volvo in 1976.

The model (which was smaller than any other Volvo before or since) was conceived as a form of personal, local transport for one or more people, complementing bigger, petrol or diesel-engined family cars.

Volvo had never intended the little electric car for series production. However, the working prototypes did fulfil two functions: they generated some valuable PR for Volvo as a maker of 'green' vehicles and they demonstrated, in practical trials, that the electric car will not become a viable option until suitable batteries have been developed!

Project 1155

Volvo's new executive model, the 760GLE, was unveiled in 1982 at the then-staggering price of SKr99,800. The new car had been developed under the codename of 'Project 1155' (leading Volvo employees to joke that the company had waited until 'five to midnight' to produce a modern successor to the venerable 140/240).

Only one version was produced initially, a four-door saloon with a complete range of features (air conditioning and a sunroof were included as standard in the basic price). It was clear, however, that a 'popular' version was to follow within a year.

The model was based on the same technical concepts as the 264GLE, including rear-wheel drive, a live rear axle and a B28 engine with a five-speed manual gearbox or automatic transmission. However, thanks to further refinement, the noise level was lower and the standard of comfort considerably higher.

The body was surprisingly conventional and 'boxy' for a new 1980s model, and the aerodynamics were far from perfect. On the other hand, the relatively upright side windows maximised the interior space and provided a feeling of roominess which was much superior to many of the model's competitors.

The V6 engine in the 760GLE was no more popular than it had been in the 264GLE; despite its relatively high rating, it lacked the power and smoothness of the six-in-line units used by its main rivals. It was to be another eight years (1990) before Volvo would have a 'straight six' which would lift its top-of-the-range model into the Mercedes-Benz and BMW class in terms of engine performance.

After a time, a considerably livelier, four-cylinder, 2.3-litre unit with a turbo and intercooler became available as a complement to the PRV V6 unit (B27) made in Douvrin, France. Another powerplant option was the six-cylinder, precombustion chamber diesel already used in the 240 series which, with a turbo, was also much livelier than the B27 and made the 760 Diesel a comfortable touring car with long refuelling intervals.

Although the four-cylinder 740 took some time to appear, this did not create major problems since modifications made to the 240 around the same time had given that model a new injection of popularity.

Far right: The estate version of the Volvo 760.

1982–92

Powered by a 2.3-litre fuel-injection engine, the 740GLE finally made its debut in 1984 as a replacement for the earlier – and extremely popular – 240GLT, which was a well-equipped, high-performance, four-cylinder model. As yet, there was no sign of a 'popular' 740.

This finally appeared a year later in the guise of the 740GL; Volvo had at last found the formula for a successful replacement for the still popular, but now elderly 240.

An estate model was added at the beginning of 1985. 'Custom-designed' for the US market (and also launched there), this quickly became a best seller thanks to the higher standard of comfort, but equally high loading capacity, which it offered in comparison with the 245 'workhorse'. The model was introduced in both 760 and 740 versions. Customers outside North America had to wait some time for the opportunity of buying a 700 series estate.

From the 1987 model year on, the more 'popular' 740 and the more 'exclusive' 760 developed along separate lines to a certain extent. The scope of the modifications made to the 760GLE was such that it might almost have been regarded as a completely new car (as Volvo maintained, with slight exaggeration, in its advertisements). Although new front styling with improved streamlining was the most obvious change, the real improvement was the new 'multilink' rear suspension. Employing an ingenious linkage system, this complicated 'split axle' arrangement combined the advantages of independent suspension (high comfort and low unsprung weight) with that of a convetional beam axle (constant track width) – a crucial advantage on winter roads. This was an epochal advance, despite the fact that a similar suspension had been used previously, for example on the British Fairthorpe TX sports car back in 1965.

The advanced rear suspension was used only on the saloon model; a conventional live axle was retained on both the 740 and 760 estates.

Overleaf: Volvo 780.

Volvo 760 saloon.

Above and facing page, bottom left: Volvo 740 estate.

Below: Volvo 740 saloon.

Both luxury 'stretch' and 'sporty' versions of the 700 series were produced in the middle and late 1980s. Both types were priced well above the 'ordinary' series-built four and five-door models.

The 760 Limousine superseded the earlier 264TE (the limousine bodies were no longer built by Bertone in Italy, but much closer to home by Yngve Nilssons Karosserifabrik in Laholm, Sweden). In addition to this model, simpler, extended versions of the 740 designed for taxi service (initially with four doors) were added to the range during the 1980s. In 1988, a six-door variant was introduced to make it easier for taxi passengers to enter and leave the vehicle.

The 780, a luxury, two-door model styled by Bertone in Italy and built in limited numbers, was introduced in 1985 as successor to the not entirely successful 262 Coupé. The new arrival came with a choice of three engine, including two different V6s – the B28 already used in the 760 and a turbo with a smaller swept volume (basically the same engine as in the Renault Alpine A310 Turbo sports car). However, the latter was never used in the production 780 due to lack of space under the attractive bonnet, which prevented efficient dissipation of the heat from the high-performance unit.

In addition to the two petrol engines, the 780 was available with the same diesel unit as the 760, now with an intercooler as well as a turbocharger and rated at 122 hp. This option was intended mainly for 'diesel' markets such as Italy and France.

In the latter years of the 780, the B28/B280 engine was complemented by the B230 Turbo, an option which offered both high performance and high fuel efficiency (but was never sold in Sweden).

The 780s were actually not the most outstanding 'high-performance' versions of the 700 series. These were to be found instead among the 740s, many of which had with stiffer suspension and surprisingly good roadholding. The 740 Turbo (a budget version of the 760 Turbo) was introduced as early as the mid-1980s, while the 740GLT16v was launched in both saloon and estate versions in 1988. This was powered by a modified 156-hp B23 engine with twin overhead camshafts and 16 valves.

The most spectacular of all 700s was a 740 sold only outside Sweden (like the PV444 with the B14A engine in its time). The B204GT power unit used in this case was a B23 downsized to 2 litres, with the same cylinder head as the 'ordinary' GLT16v (i.e. with twin overhead cams and 16 valves), but with the addition of a turbo and intercooler. With 200 hp under the bonnet, this 740 was an extremely fast car! Unfortunately for Swedish enthusiasts, national emission control standards prevented this variant from being marketed at home.

The Volvo 740 was also built for professional use (such as this six-door version).

Below: The Volvo 740 saloon pictured in an elegant French setting.

Introduced as a VIP model, the 760 Executive was a luxurious, extended version of the 760GLE. The model offered excellent legroom to the rear seat passenger who could afford the luxury of a personal chauffeur, and who did not need the folding seats installed in the 760 Limousine. Like the latter (and the taxi versions), the 760 Executive was built by Nilssons in Laholm.

In 1990, the 760 was succeeded by the considerably more refined 960. However, the 740 remained in production for a further two years as a somewhat more basic alternative to the 940.

Model	Period of manufacture	Number built	Wheelbase cm	Track width (front/rear), cm	Swept volume, cm³	Engine rating, hp	No. of forward speeds
760 saloon	1982–90	183,864	277	147/146–152	2,316–2,849	109–182	5 (A)
740 saloon	1984–92	650,443	277	147/146	1,986–2,383	82–200	5 (A)
760 estate	1985–90	37,445	277	147/151	2,316–2,849	109–182	5 (A)
740 estate	1985–92	358,952	277	147/151	1,986–2,383	82–200	5 (A)
780	1985–90	8,518	277	147/146–152	2,316–2,849	129–170	5 (A)

World's lightest Volvo

Volvo has presented its own concept of an ecological car of the future every decade since the 1970s. Each concept has been different.

The 1983 LCP (Light Component Project) was a more ambitious venture than the two electric cars seven years before. The vehicle in question was a four-seater car with unlimited range, and with speed and acceleration resources comparable to those of a conventional model.

The model featured front-wheel drive. Although this was a radical innovation for Volvo at the time, it was to be a common feature on Volvo cars within the not too distant future.

Unlike the previous experimental vehicles, the 'heart' of the LCP was an internal combustion engine in the form of a specially developed three-cylinder, direct-injection diesel (a type which had not yet been used in any production model). Volvo's ability to develop a small unit of this type was no accident; apart from its successful development work on efficient diesels in bigger sizes for trucks and buses, it had been producing small, direct-injection

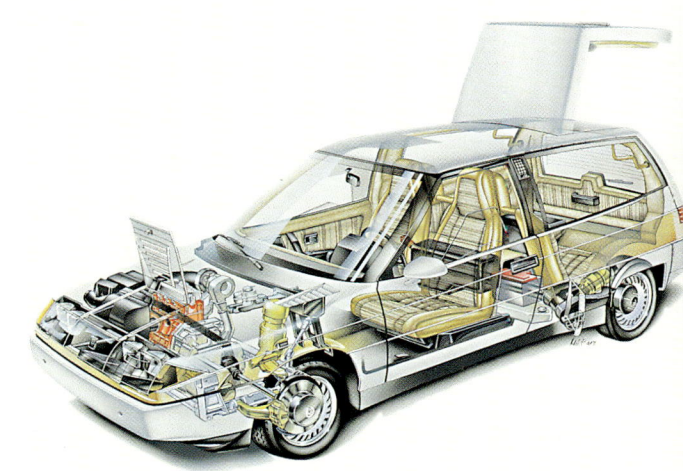

diesels for small boats since the introduction of its revolutionary single-cylinder MD1 (Marine Diesel 1) unit in New York in 1958.

Despite its very low fuel consumption, the extremely light, turbocharged engine used in the LCP developed more than sufficient power to propel the streamlined model at speeds well in excess of legal motorway limits.

The interior space in the aerodynamically styled body was optimised for four occupants by seating the rear-seat passengers facing the rear, perhaps the most dubious feature of what was otherwise a fully production-ready design.

However, the most innovative aspect of the LCP was the choice of materials used in its construction. To minimise the energy required to drive it, most of the vehicle was built from extremely light materials, including magnesium in the engine and many other major components. Glass fibre-reinforced plastic was another material which was used extensively. As a result, the vehicle had an extremely low kerb weight, which was well below that of any previous car in its size class or any model with the LCP's functional attributes.

1983

The fact that the LCP was a fully working and practical car, rather than just an experimental model, was amply demonstrated by the comprehensive test programme which it underwent and in which it was test-driven, among others, by a large number of journalists. The model received universal praise and there were many who regretted that it would never reach the marketplace in its concept form.

Designed under the direction of Rolf Mellde (formerly of Saab), the LCP was important as an inspiration in the future development of efficient, front-wheel drive Volvo cars.

Springboard

Bottom right: The Volvo 480 was produced in relatively small numbers.

Below: High-tech methods, such as robots, were used to produce the 400 series.

The 400 series represented a new departure for Volvo. Rear-wheel drive was now replaced by front-wheel drive, the engine was mounted transversely, and performance and handling received high priority. It was a new approach which was to result in the development of Volvo cars with sportier characteristics.

The 480 was presented as a new Volvo sports car on its introduction in 1985 (as the 1986 model). This was both correct and incorrect – correct because the handling was excellent, but incorrect because the model, despite its outward appearance, provided adequate space for four occupants, even for tall passengers in the rear.

However, with a 1.8-litre Renault engine developing barely 100 hp under the bonnet, the model's performance did not match its looks. Although the speed resources were greatly improved by the subsequent introduction of a turbo version, they remained unexceptional.

Volvo's decision to launch the most exclusive variant of the 400 series first was certainly no coincidence; the company wanted its image to 'rub off' on the more mundane four-door versions due to be introduced three to fours years later. In the event, however, the 480 suffered from severe growing pains, just like the 343 a decade or so before. These included problems of all types, from electrical faults in the sophisticated electronics to cracks in the big rear window (a feature influenced by the spectacular rear-end design of the 1800ES over a decade earlier).

The 480 remained a fairly exclusive car which was sold in relatively small numbers, providing the engineers with an opportunity of correcting the

1985–96

various design faults before the 440 and 460 were unveiled in 1988 and 1989.

Like all Dutch-built Volvos, the 480 boasted superb handling (which had helped DAF cars to achieve several victories over much tougher competition, both on the track and in rally events). This, together with its lavish standard equipment (especially in the 480 Turbo), made it beloved of owners who enjoyed driving.

The four-door 440 – a variant which was destined to be the most important in the model family – appeared in 1988. Distinguished by its foreshortened rear end, this was intended as a small, medium-class car with sufficient space for a family, but with the manoeuvrability necessary in built-up urban areas in which parking was a perennial problem. The model was of practical design, with an opening rear hatch and the sloped rear end which was (and is) the preference of the great majority of European motorists.

Despite its qualities, the 440 never became a top-seller. This may have been due to the fact that although it was a good car in most respects, it was not unique or outstanding in any one. Nevertheless, with 120 hp under the bonnet and top-class handling characteristics, the turbo version, in particular, was something of a wolf in sheep's clothing.

Since the model's stubby rear end was not to everybody's taste, its sibling, the 460, was introduced in 1990. This featured more conservative rear-end styling with a conventional – and much more spacious – boot. In terms of its technical specifications, the 460 was identical to both the 480 and the 440.

The Volvo 460 (above left), 440 (above) and 480 (left).

Overleaf: The Volvo 480 cabriolet prototype which was unveiled in 1990.

Model	Period of manufacture	Number built	Wheelbase, cm	Track width (front/rear), cm	Swept volume, cm^3	Engine rating, hp	No. of forward speeds
480	1985–95	76,375	250	142/143	1,721–1,998	95–120	5 (A)
440	1988–96	384,682	250	142/143	1,596–1,998	79–120	5 (A)
460	1989–96	238,401	250	142/143	1,596–1,998	82–120	5 (A)

End of an era

The 940 was based on its predecessor, the 740. Together with a more lavish standard of equipment, the new styling made it the best-selling car in Sweden.

Far right: Turbocharging (which was eventually to become a standard feature) made the 940 a high-performance car.

A new generation of Swedish Volvos appeared in 1990 in the form of the 900 series. This was essentially a refined version of the still-modern 700 series, but with gentler lines. Like all big Volvos before, the new models were naturally equipped with rear-wheel drive (although those who believed that this was a permanent Volvo feature were in for a surprise a year or so later).

The new 900 series consisted of eight different body options – the 960 executive, limousine, saloon, estate and ambulance, and the 940 saloon, taxi (six-door) and estate.

In comparison with the 760, which it had finally replaced, the 960 boasted a whole range of new features and modifications.

The most obvious change compared with the 740 (which remained in production for another year in parallel with the new series) was the softer, restyled roofline of the saloon. In other respects, the body was generally unchanged, except for a more elegant front and new, more modern headlamps.

The most exciting new feature was the new, six-cylinder engine with double overhead camshafts and four valves per cylinder. Made entirely of aluminium (to save weight), the unit also had an extremely short overall length (thanks to the short spacing between the cylinders and the unusual 'long-stroke' configuration).

Initially, the 960 was built only in a 3-litre version. A 2.5-litre 'budget' version was introduced later, while a variant with an even smaller engine was produced for a limited number of markets.

The 960 was not produced as a diesel – this was a car for people who could afford the fuel...

Under the skin, the differences between the 960 and 940 were greater than they appeared. The front end of the 960 had been completely redesigned, both to accommodate the new engine and to improve ride comfort. The 960 estate was provided with a modified version of the multilink rear suspension introduced in the 760 saloon back in 1986, whereas the 940 was equipped with the same conventional rear suspension throughout its life.

The 960 boasted much more luxurious interior appointments than the 940.

Both models offered the same high standard of

safety as their predecessors, the 760 and 740. Passive safety was improved even further when the series was equipped with the patented side-impact protection system (SIPS) first used in the new 850 in 1991.

For executive and professional applications, the series was augmented successively by more or less the same body options as the 760/740 (but with a more attractive roofline). The Executive and Limousine bodies built by Nilssons in Laholm, in particular, boasted a standard of luxury and elegance never before seen in a Volvo. This was especially true of the Executive, which was equipped with luxurious, individual armchairs in the rear instead of the usual style of rear seat.

However, the days of the rear-wheel drive cars built in Gothenburg were numbered, and it was only a matter of time before they gave way to their successor, the S80. Before that, however, the 960 saloon had been renamed the 'S90' and the 960 estate the 'V90'. The 940, on the other hand, retained its designation until the end of its production life.

The last 940/S90/V90 cars left the line at the beginning of 1998 as perhaps the last rear wheel-drive Volvos to be built. An era had ended and a new one was about to begin.

The estate became the most popular version of the 940.

End of an era: The last rear-wheel drive Volvo leaves the plant.

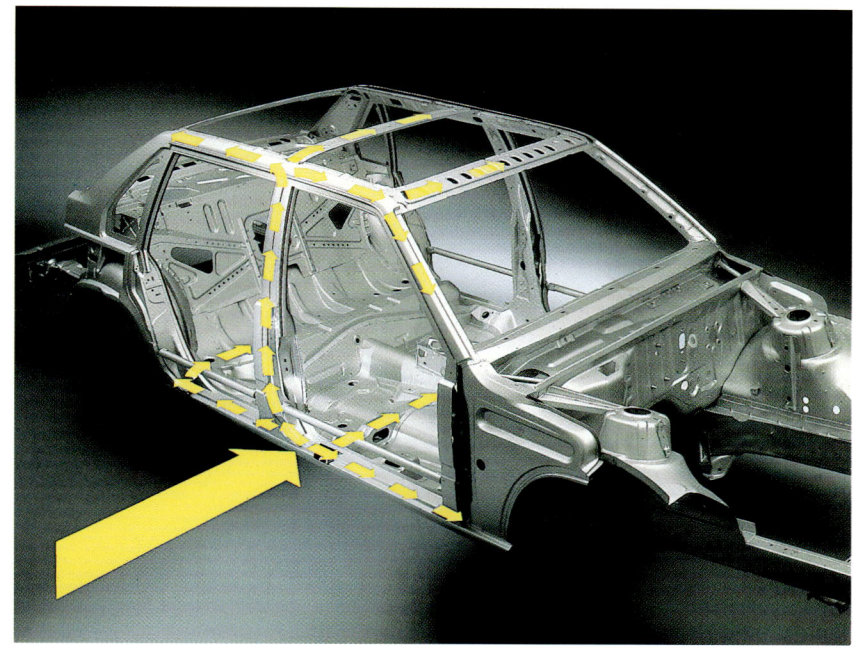

Above left: SIPS – Volvo's revolutionary side impact protection system – has saved many lives.

Top right: The front of the 960 was restyled in 1994, improving the aerodynamics.

Left: A more impressive car could hardly be imagined. A 'super' version of the Volvo 960 with a four-cylinder, turbocharged, 16-valve, 200-hp engine pictured in Volvo's showrooms on the Champs Elysées in Paris.

Facing page: The Volvo 960 in a winter setting.

Model	Period of manufacture	Number built	Wheelbase, cm	Track width (front/rear), cm	Swept volume, cm^3	Engine rating, hp	No. of forward speeds
940 saloon	1990–98	246,704	277	147/146	1,986–2,383	82–200	5 (A)
940 estate	1990–98	231,677	277	147/146	1,986–2,383	82–200	5 (A)
960 saloon	1990–96	112,710	277	150/152	2,473–2,922	170–204	5 (A)
960 estate	1990–96	41,619	277	150/152	2,473–2,922	170–204	5 (A)
S90	1996–98	26,269	277	150/152	2,922	182–204	5 (A)
V90	1996–98	9,067	277	150/152	2,922	182–204	5 (A)

New generation

Far right and facing page, top left: Volvo's five-cylinder, in-line engine with double overhead camshafts was also available in a Bi-Fuel version with excellent environmental performance.

Bottom right: The 850 was safer than any previous Volvo thanks to the unique SIPS system (seen undergoing test).

Below: With front-wheel drive and sporty handling characteristics, the Volvo 850 represented a new departure for the company.

Volvo resisted the clear trend towards front-wheel drive for many years. In 1991, however, it was time to lift the veil on the company's first model of that type.

The 850 received a warmer reception than perhaps any other previous car in Volvo's history (with the exception of the PV444). Motoring journalists enthused (unfairly!) that Volvo had at last built a car which was "actually fun to drive".

Undeniably, however, the model did represent a completely new trend in Volvo's big, Swedish-built cars. Here, for the first time, was a genuinely high-performance model with handling qualities which enabled its generous power resources to be exploited.

The most radical innovation was the front-wheel drive and transverse engine configuration. This had necessitated the development of a completely new engine generation (the first, six-cylinder variant of which had been used in the 960 the previous year, although mounted longitudinally in the 'conventional' manner and driving the rear

wheels). The five-cylinder, in-line unit in the 850 was designed with a very short overall length to enable it to be installed transversely (Volvo's experience of the vee-type was far from positive given the problems encountered with the PRV unit).

– 102 –

1991–

The S70, which replaced the 850, was characterised by a redesigned rear end and softer front-end styling.

The engine was of the latest design, with double overhead camshafts and four valves per cylinder. The powerful GLT version of the 2.5-litre unit (the only option available at the start) developed 170 hp, giving a top speed of well over 200 km/h.

Several more engine options – both 'upward' and 'downward' – were added in time. These included a version with two valves per cylinder for a less expensive 850 variant. In addition, a 2-litre version (not to be confused with the four-cylinder unit of the same family used in the 40 series) was introduced for markets in which cars over two litres are subject to taxation penalties and for price-sensitive customers in other countries.

The 2-litre engine was available initially in both four and two-valve versions; however, all 2-litre units became four-valve from the 1999 model year on.

With the introduction of the 850 Turbo (and its high-performance sibling, the T5-R), customers had their first opportunity of buying a Volvo capable of a top speed of 250 km/h – road conditions and speed limits permitting! Suddenly, the Volvo 850 was a candidate even for the fast lane on the German autobahns!

In the area of safety, Volvo was the first carmaker in the world to introduce a brand-new, integrated system of protection against lateral collisions. The innovation in question was SIPS (Side Impact Protection System), which improved the occupants' chances of emerging unscathed even from a serious incident of this type.

Initially, the 850 was available only as a saloon, whose relatively discreet styling revealed its

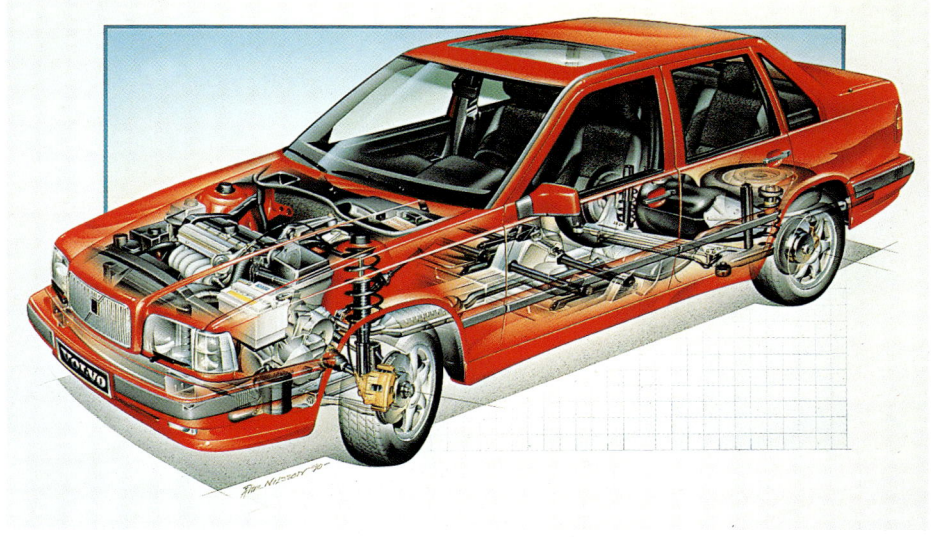

The new Volvo 850 boasted a series of technical innovations.

Previous pages: For the first time, the yellow, high-performance version of the 850 made Volvo a prime choice for speed lovers. Far right: The successor to the high-performance version.

Below and facing page, bottom left: Equipped with all-wheel drive, the most spectacular version of the V70 – the V70 XC 'Cross Country' – delivers improved mobility and high performance.

relationship with the 440/460 family. A second body option, the 850 estate, with its characteristic vertical and highly visible rear lights, followed at the beginning of 1993 – and became just as popular as the saloon.

With the 850, Volvo had successfully broken into the second highest division among performance cars (it had no plans to break the 300 km/h barrier). Journalists and customers alike were even more enthused by the appearance of the famous 850 T-5R – a fully equipped, 250-hp version of both the saloon and estate, with a stiffer suspension, a distinctive pale yellow finish and matching leather upholstery.

A diesel version with a five-cylinder, transversely mounted Volkswagen engine had already been introduced in 1996 for economy-minded customers. This offered a unique combination of extremely high fuel efficiency and a top speed of about 200 km/h.

New versions of the normally-aspirated petrol engines, with significantly lower fuel consumption,

were introduced in 1999 to the delight of thrifty drivers who prefer petrol engines to diesels. Even the lowest-powered units now had four valves per cylinder and the Volvo plant in Skövde had produced its last two-valve petrol engine.

The top-class qualities of the 850 chassis were

– 106 –

amply demonstrated by Rickard Rydell's bravura performances in the car (first in the estate and later in the four-door version) for Tom Walkinshaw's TWR stable in the British Touring Car Championship. The cooperation between Volvo and TWR in the BTCC led to the development of the attractive, high-performance C70 Coupé and C70 Convertible, both of which are built in a plant owned jointly by the two companies in Uddevalla, Sweden.

Volvo unveiled a four-wheel drive version of the 850 (initially only as an estate) in 1996, endowing what was already a superb winter car with even better winter driving characteristics and improved mobility. With its limited ground clearance, the 850 AWD was not, however, a true terrain vehicle.

In 1997, the company launched what was essentially a further developed 850 under the designations 'S70' and 'V70', analogous to those of the S40/V40 models which had already been introduced. In both cases, 'S' stood for 'Saloon' (or 'Sedan') and 'V' for 'Versatility'. The most obvious innovations were a completely new, aerodynamic front and a new rear end in the four-door version.

The V70 AWD replaced the 850 AWD at the same time. For AWD enthusiasts who preferred a four-door model, the S70 became available with this feature some time later. Another later addition was the V70 XC ('Cross Country'), whose considerably higher ground clearance gave it better terrain mobility.

Above: Volvo proved to be both a surprise and a sensation when it began to compete in the tough British Touring Car Championship with the estate version of the 850.

Left: Introduced in 1993, the 850 estate combined familiar Volvo lines with a new, softer image.

Model	Period of manufacture	Number built	Wheelbase, cm	Track width (front/rear), cm	Swept volume, cm³	Engine rating, hp	No. of forward speeds
850 saloon	1991–97	390,727	266	152/147	1,984–2,460	126–250	5 (A)
850 estate	1993–97	326,703	266	152/147	1,984–2,460	126–250	5 (A)
S70	1996–		266	152/147	1,984–2,460	122–250	5 (A)
V70	1996–		266	152/147	1,984–2,460	122–265	5 (A)

Ecological high-tech

Far right: A gas turbine enabled the ECC hybrid car to run on all fuels, including renewable and 'green' types.

The cockpit in the ECC was not only comfortable and safe; it boasted every conceivable aid, such as a GPS navigation system.

The Volvo ECC (Environmental Concept Car) was unveiled in 1992 as the third of Volvo's proposals for an ecological car of the future (after the 1976 electric car and the 1983 LCP). Even more functional than the two previous concepts, the latest design was comparable or superior to an 'ordinary' car in all respects, and boasted exciting, individual lines which were to be reflected in the Volvo S80 five years later.

The ECC was a conventional four-door saloon. On this occasion, the designers drew on the body of expertise available within the Volvo Group as a whole to design a state-of-the-art power unit which was not only extremely light, but ran equally well on all fuels, whether finite (like oil) or renewable. A gas turbine was chosen for this purpose.

A gas turbine had never before been used in a series-built car. (The sole exception was in 1964, when Chrysler had produced a series of 50 elegant, gas turbine-driven cars with expensive, handcrafted Italian bodies; however, almost all of these were

scrapped on completion of the test programme to avoid paying import duties on the bodies.) In practice, the speed of the gas turbine is too high to drive a conventional transmission; however, it is ideal in a hybrid drive.

As a matter of historical record, the ECC was not the first working gas-turbine model built by Volvo. As far back as the 1970s, Sven-Olof Kronogård (the technical genius who was head of the United Turbine company at the time) had demonstrated a fully operational 264 prototype with a Volvo-designed gas turbine under the bonnet.

Volvo had (and has) extensive experience of gas turbines through Volvo Aero Corporation and its subsidiary, United Turbine of Malmö, which developed the ECC powerplant.

The ECC was a hybrid car – a type which uses two basically different power sources, in this case an electric motor to propel the vehicle and a gas turbine driving a generator to produce energy for a bank of on-board batteries.

In one sense, therefore, the model was an electric car like its 1976 forerunner. The difference now was that the new model afforded a combination of zero-emission operation over short distances (in battery-only mode) and unlimited range (powered by the gas turbine). Running continuously, the gas

1992

turbine could supply sufficient power to drive the electric motor at a constantly high output.

The electric motor is superior to the internal combustion engine in one respect: its torque curve is practically linear (in other words, it is equally high at all speeds). As a result, only a very simple transmission (or, in some cases, none at all) is required.

The gas turbine and electric motor share one characteristic: they are both extremely light, making them ideal for use in vehicles.

The ECC was a widely publicised and much appreciated car. As before, however, it was essentially a concept rather than a model destined for production within the foreseeable future. Its development was part of a Group-wide project which culminated in the appearance of Volvo Truck Corporation's ECT (Environmental Concept Truck) and Volvo Bus Corporation's ECB (Environmental Concept Bus) about two years later.

The ECC's power unit was not its only economic feature. In addition to its many other innovations, it was built for almost 100% recycling at the end of its useful life, enabling other new, environmentally compatible products to be made from the original materials.

An everyday racer

All photographs on these pages are of the Volvo S40.

Volvo is now a carmaker with access to the enormous development resources of Ford, guaranteeing that its future models will continue to embody the company's traditional core values of quality, safety and environmental care. The situation was different when the time came to develop a medium-class car to succeed the 400 series; at that time Volvo did not command the resources and production volume required to develop its 'own' model in what is a highly competitive class.

The solution was found in a joint venture with Mitsubishi, the Japanese carmaker, which has a distinguished record in technical innovation (for example, the balance shaft arrangement used in the B234 engine in the Volvo 740GLT16v is a Mitsubishi patent).

The joint venture with Mitsubishi was the last major agreement to be concluded by Pehr G. Gyllenhammar before he was forced to resign from Volvo following the abandonment of the proposed

1995

merger with Renault (which, in reality, would have been a takeover by the French company).

Although the 400 series had been something of a success, it had not been produced in the high numbers required to enable Volvo to develop its own successor to its first series-built, front-wheel drive family. The answer was to join with Mitsubishi in developing a new 'platform' forming the basis for

Rickard Rydell (pictured on left) made the S40 famous as a competition car when he won the British Touring Car Championship in his five-cylinder version.

both a new Volvo (S40/V40) and a new Mitsubishi (the Carisma).

From the beginning, it was clear that the concept involved a completely new philosophy. The cars were not only to be developed by separate, competitive carmakers, but were to be built in the same (now jointly-owned) plant at Born in the Netherlands.

The development work was carried out in parallel by the two companies. Despite the common platform, the two models were completely different in appearance and, to some extent, in character. Whereas Mitsubishi opted for a four-door saloon and a hatchback, Volvo chose to develop two different bodies, a classic four-door saloon (S40) and a functional estate car (V40).

the diesel versions have become extremely popular in central Europe, especially with the replacement (in 1999) of the precombustion chamber engine used in the first versions by a modern, fuel-efficient, direct-injection type made (as before) by Renault. Economy-minded motorists who do not want a diesel have the option of Mitsubishi's renowned direct-injection petrol engine, a unit which delivers appreciably lower fuel consumption than a 'conventional' petrol engine, if not quite as low as a diesel.

The S40/V40 has remained basically unchanged since its introduction, except that the turbo version is now recognisable by the elegant and efficient headlamps of new design. Since 1998, these have also been available as an extra on other S40/V40 models.

Whereas earlier Dutch-built Volvos were sold in a limited number of countries, the S40/V40 has become a 'world' car to a large extent, especially since its introduction in North America in summer 1999.

The end products were two attractive models which slotted perfectly into the compact medium class – a popular size of car almost everywhere in the world.

However, the functional aspect soon took a back seat as it became clear that this was not 'just' a Volvo with traditional qualities of safety and comfort. What Volvo had created was a compact, high-performance car capable of assuming the mantle of the legendary PV544 Sport, which had won laurels in both the racing and rallying arenas.

The S40 (and the slightly later V40) was launched with a choice of two 16-valve engines, with ratings of 1.8 and 2 litres respectively, both made by Volvo in Skövde. With the introduction of the S40/V40 T4 with a 200-hp engine (and the same gearbox as in the 70 series), it became clear that Volvo was at last offering a tigerish, high-performance car (actually two) with practical features, at a price within the reach of most new car buyers.

The excellent handling characteristics of the Volvo S40 were confirmed when Rickard Rydell won the 1998 British Touring Car Championship in the model. Although built on basically the same chassis as the standard version, his car was a refined racing version with the five-cylinder, 2-litre engine from the 850/S70 under the bonnet.

The S40/V40 are versatile models. As a result,

The model pictured on these pages is the Volvo V40.

Model	Period of manufacture	Number built	Wheelbase, cm	Track width (front/rear), cm	Swept volume, cm^3	Engine rating, hp	No. of forward speeds
S40	1995–		255	145/147	1,587–1,948	90–200	5 (A)
V40	1996–		255	145/147	1,587–1,948	90–200	5 (A)

Two noble beauties

Volvo has always built safe, robust cars, and the term 'flamboyant' has never really been associated with them. In 1996, however, this assessment had to be revised when the C70 appeared.

The first version to be unveiled was the C70 Coupé. This was the first series-built model to emerge from Volvo's cooperation with Tom Walkinshaw Racing (TWR), the British company which had been in charge of Volvo's activities in the British Touring Car Championship since 1994.

Having created cars such as the Jaguar XJ220 and the Aston Martin DB7 – both built as very small series – Tom Walkinshaw must have been highly gratified by the reception accorded the Volvo C70 Coupé at the Paris Motor Show in October 1996. The attractive new car aroused great interest, not only for its beautiful lines and the unusual finishes in which it was presented, but also for the fact that it was to be built in a plant jointly owned by the two companies in Uddevalla, Sweden.

The Volvo C70 Coupé was based on the successful front-wheel drive chassis used in the 70 series. The

1996–

technical equipment was also from the 850/S70, including the 240-hp turbo engine, which delivered a top speed of 250 km/h. The quality of the model's roadholding matched its speed and acceleration.

Despite its performance, it was the car's styling, luxurious interior, materials, ergonomics and comfort which won the hearts of journalists and all other visitors to the Volvo stand at the Paris show.

Finished in leather and wood (with patterned aluminium as an option), the C70 Coupé accommodates four people in luxurious comfort. The rear seat is designed in the form of two comfortable armchairs.

In truth, the overwhelming reception which the C70 Coupé received may not have been due entirely to its qualities, but to the fact that this was the model the public had expected from a Swedish manufacturer with a tradition of leadership in safety.

Despite the longings which it aroused among the public and prospective buyers, it was some time before deliveries of the model commenced in earnest. The engineering quality standards applied by Volvo on this occasion were particularly high and production – which was largely of a handcraft nature – was limited accordingly.

The C70 Coupé will never be a common sight on the roads. But to the driver who enjoys driving rather than merely travelling by car, it offers a perfect compromise between high speed, maximum safety and superb styling on the one hand, and the comfort and spaciousness of a four-seater on the other.

The C70 Coupé (which was a fixed head model) was followed about a year later by what was originally known as a 'drophead' (or convertible), an open-top car with the convenience of wind-down windows and a folding hood offering at least the same protection against the weather as a metal roof. This version was named the C70 Convertible.

The photographs on these and the following pages are of the Volvo C70 Coupé.

The decision to introduce the C70 Convertible was influenced particularly by demands from North American customers, who wanted an open-top car with the inherent qualities of a Volvo.

Volvo had produced open-top models on several previous occasions, beginning with the company's very first car (pages 14-17). Sophisticated cabriolets were also built on the PV655 (page 23) and PV445 (pages 50-51) chassis, not to mention the 'plastic' P1900 sports car (pages 52-55).

For safety reasons, Volvo had consciously refrained from producing open cars for many years. However, equipped with a newly developed Volvo system known as ROPS (Roll-Over Protection System), ABS brakes and a driver airbag, the C70 Convertible was as safe as any model of its type could possibly be.

The C70 Convertible is more than just a beautiful car; it is also a fast, high-performance machine with a top speed of up to 250 km/h. Not for nothing was it developed jointly by Volvo and TWR,

All pictures on these pages are of the Volvo C70 Convertible.

which not only manages Volvo's involvement in the BTCC racing series, but has also won the Le Mans 24-hour rally on several occasions in its own cars (and is involved in Formula 1 with the Arrows team). Different engine options from 165 to 240 hp are available depending on the customer's requirements, although even the lowest-rated of these should more than satisfy most enthusiasts (open-top driving is at its most enjoyable at speeds below 200 km/h).

Despite its performance, the C70 Convertible is also a practical car, with an electrically operated fabric hood which is adequately insulated against arctic winter conditions. While the luggage compartment is not, perhaps, as spacious as that in a Volvo estate, it does accommodate the lucky driver's golf clubs and weekend baggage (and those of his or her passengers).

Ultimately, however, it is neither its performance nor its practicality which first impresses the beholder; the model's most striking quality is its beauty.

With the hood down the C70 Convertible's 'standard equipment' includes four sources of noise: wind noise, engine noise and road noise – and the sound of the ten loudspeakers included in the state-of-the-art audio system.

The C70 Convertible can hardly be described as the most 'sensible' car in the Volvo range. However, it is the most fun – and the one most likely to attract envious glances on the road!

Model	Period of manufacture	Number built	Wheelbase, cm	Track width (front/rear), cm	Swept volume, cm^3	Engine rating, hp	No. of forward speeds
C70 Coupé	1996–		266	152/151	1,984–2,435	165–240	5 (A)
C70 Convertible	1997–		266	152/151	2,435	165–240	5 (A)

World's safest car!

In summer 1999, the Volvo S80 became the first car in history to win the highest rating of five stars in the crash test carried out by the reputable National Highway Transport Safety Authority (NHTSA) in the USA. Volvo had finally achieved official recognition as maker of the safest cars in the world!

This historic distinction provided welcome acknowledgement that the model launched by Volvo in 1998 was something very special.

In spring 1998, it was clear to the people of Gothenburg that something was afoot. The newspapers reported that Volvo had hired the Gothenburg Opera, while the roof of a nearby city-centre building was decorated with the attractive outline of a car in the shape of a safety pin. Meanwhile, over a period of several months, thousands of Volvo personnel from all over the world

were receiving information on the development and engineering of Volvo's best and safest car ever – the S80.

The S80 was a further development of the successful formula used in the S40/V40, C70 and S70/V70 – front-wheel drive with a transversely mounted, in-line engine, a high standard of safety, generous interior space for the car's class, excellent handling and top-class performance. The model also included several world 'firsts', showing that a small, independent Swedish carmaker could hold its own among the world's leading marques in terms of technology.

On this occasion, the styling was unusually daring, inspired as it was by the 1992 ECC. The angular lines which had characterised all recent Volvo cars (except the S40/V40 and C70) since 1982 were consciously eliminated, not only improving the aerodynamics but signifying a break with the past and the arrival of a new, more fluid Volvo shape. The design was a clear statement that Volvo intended to develop its own distinctive image for the future.

The bonnet of the S80 concealed a transversely mounted, straight six engine – a unique configuration which was achieved by designing an

1998–

The photographs on these and the following pages are of the Volvo S80.

extremely compact unit and making the car relatively wide (with the added advantage of maximising the interior space).

Initially, the S80 came with two different six-cylinder powerplants. The first was a high-powered 272-hp turbo (the most powerful unit ever built by Volvo) delivering an electronically limited top speed of 250 km/h. , The second was a normally-aspirated version of the same unit with a higher swept volume, developing 200 hp and delivering 'only' 235 km/h.

Several other engine options, from the same direct-injection diesel used in the S70/V70 to a five-cylinder, 2-litre turbo, were introduced at the same time.

These were complemented by a series of new and extremely compact manual and automatic gearboxes, which enabled the big in-line engines to be installed transversely in the engine compartment.

The S80 is equipped with a highly advanced electrical system based on multiplex technology to ensure total control of all on-board electrical functions. The system is controlled by up to 18 microprocessors, which monitor the various functions more quickly and more precisely than earlier systems.

Safety was central to the model's development. In addition to accepted Volvo features, such as ABS brakes, airbags and SIPS, standard equipment in the S80 includes WHIPS, a unique design of front seat which affords protection against whiplash injuries in rear-end impacts, and a special inflatable curtain offering the occupants improved protection in side collisions.

However, apart from its effects on its occupants, a car has an impact on the environment at large. As a result, every S80 is accompanied by a comprehensive environmental product declaration (EPD) certified by Lloyd's Register Quality Assurance in London. The EPD describes the overall environmental impact of the model from its design and production, through its useful life, to its final disposal, including the recovery and recycling of its materials to manufacture new cars or other useful products.

The innovative aspects of the S80 were not confined to its technical features; the organisation behind its development and production in Gothenburg also underwent radical change. To achieve total control over the entire production system, Volvo selected suppliers and partners located close to the production plant, and many of the model's components are manufactured and assembled in an industrial park on the island of Hisingen itself. This enables all of the parts to be manufactured, inspected and assembled with perfect precision.

The S80 will remain the company's prestige model well into the next century, and is certain to have a significant influence on the design of future Volvo cars.

Model	Period of manufacture	Number built	Wheelbase, cm	Track width (front/rear), cm	Swept volume, cm^3	Engine rating, hp	No. of forward speeds
S80	1998–		279	158/156	1,984–2,922	140–272	5 (A)

Volvo 2000

The decision facing a Volvo buyer in the company's first year of operations (1927) was a simple one. Just two models were available: the PV4, if the choice was a comfortable, enclosed car, and the ÖV4 (in an attractive dark-blue finish), if an elegant, open-top model was preferred.

Faced with a whole range of model series, today's buyer has a much tougher decision. Furthermore, each product family usually comes with a number of body options.

Power units include both petrol and diesel engines with different numbers of cylinders and different ratings, with or without turbocharging.

Manual gearboxes are available to drivers who prefer manual gearchanging, with automatic transmissions for those who do not.

Bodies are supplied in a wide range of different finishes, while interiors (with fabric or leather trim) are also available in a large number of options.

Nevertheless, the Volvo range is very clearly structured, consisting of the 40, 70 and 80 families, with their own individual characteristics. Each series also includes a large number of versions and variants, each designed to meet the specific demands of a potential Volvo driver.

However, the main characteristics of the hundreds and thousands of cars which leave the company's production plants every year remain the same. Each one of these vehicles bears the hallmarks of comfort, ergonomics, safety and environmental care on which all of Volvo's carmaking activities are founded.

Characterised by quality, reliability and durability, Volvos are now perhaps the longest-lasting cars in the world.

2000

Given Volvo's concern for the environment, its cars are designed for the lowest possible exhaust emission levels. Volvo cars are also quiet (both inside and out), while the plants in which they are built are designed to minimise the impact of production operations on the neighbouring environment.

Although closely related to their forerunners, the Volvo cars of today have been refined in every respect. Levels of active and passive safety are even higher, while every model delivers higher mileage for every gallon of petrol and environmental impact has been reduced. Today's models deliver faster acceleration and top speeds which, to use a time-worn phrase, may be described as 'adequate'.

Only 297 cars, all built at Volvo's Hisingen factory, were sold in 1927. By the year 2000, production will have reached about half a million.

Volvo is one of the world's smallest marques. As such, it has the flexibility needed to respond to and take account of the needs of the individual customer.

However, Volvo is also an important part of the worldwide Ford Motor Company, assuring it of the stability and resources needed to ensure that its cars

will be even safer, more comfortable, more environmentally compatible and more fuel-efficient in future. Conversely, Ford cars will benefit from the unique automaking knowhow and experience gathered over the years by generations of Volvo people.

This volume has dealt with the first threequarters of Volvo's first century. There is no doubt that the rest of that century will be equally exciting!

The pictures on these and the following pages show the Volvos which will be produced as the year 2000 models.

Model	Model year	Body type	Wheelbase, cm	Track width (front/rear) cm	Swept volume, cm³	Engine rating, hp	No. of forward speeds
S40	2000	Saloon	255	145/147	1,587–1,948	95–200	5 (A)
V40	2000	Estate	255	145/147	1,587–1,948	95–200	5 (A)
S70	2000	Saloon	266	152/147	1,984–2,460	122–250	5 (A)
V70	2000	Estate	266	152/147	1,984–2,460	122–265	5 (A)
C70 Coupé	2000	Coupé	266	152/152	1,984–2,435	165–240	5 (A)
C70 Convertible	2000	Convertible	266	152/152	2,435	165–240	5 (A)
S80	2000	Saloon	279	158/156	1,984–2,922	140–272	5 (A)

A new model for a new millennium

A front-wheel drive version of the new V70 was unveiled in at the 2000 Detroit Motor Show, followed by a rugged AWD 'Cross Country' (XC) version in Geneva. Both attracted the plaudits of the motoring press.

With a choice of engines from 140 to 250 hp, the V70 is fast, spacious, comfortable and safe. Its many new features include a unique triple-split rear seat in the XC.

The V70 boasts an extremely high standard of safety, thanks to innovations such as WHIPS (which prevents whiplash injuries) and an inflatable side-collision curtain.

With features such as PremAir® – a method of converting ground-level ozone into oxygen at an efficiency of up to 75% – the V70 is a trail-blazer in environmental terms.